content

 **CHAPTER 1: United Nations**   5

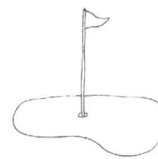 **CHAPTER 2: Sport**   40

 **CHAPTER 3: Weird as**   49

 **CHAPTER 4: One-liners**   79

 **CHAPTER 5: Q & A**   107

Volume 2

Lily Burgess

Illustrations by Dyan Burgess

National Library of Australia Cataloguing-in-Publication entry
Creator: Burgess, Lily, author.
Title: 101 of the Best Kids' Jokes Ever. Vol. 2 / Lily Burgess; Dyan Burgess.

ISBN: 978-1-925181-92-0 (paperback)
ISBN: 978-1-925181-93-7 (ebook : Kindle)
ISBN: 978-1-925181-94-4 (ebook : epub)

Target Audience: For primary school age.
Subjects: Wit and humor, Juvenile.
Other Creators/Contributors: Burgess, Dyan, illustrator.
Dewey Number: A827.4

© Lily Burgess 2015. This book is copyrighted by Lily Burgess, no part of this publication may be reproduced or transmitted in any form by any means, electronically or mechanically, including photocopy, without permission in writing from the publisher.

When you use single photo/image on social media or for reviewing could you please mention one of our links:
website www.wordsfromdaddysmouth.com.au
instagram @wordsfromdaddysmouth
or twitter @wordsfromdaddys

This is a work of fiction. Any similarity to persons living or dead is merely coincidental.

Published by D & M Fancy Pastry Pty Ltd

Typefaces: Body – Calibri Regular
           Titles – Calibri Bold

Important disclaimer
Without limiting the rights under copyright reserved above, no part of this publication may be reproduced, stored, or transmitted in any form or by any means, without prior written permission of both the copyright owner and the above publisher of this book.

The information in this book is of a general nature and is intended to be (at least for some) humorous. It is not intended to be professional advice.

The book is a collection of jokes provided to the author over time and no offence is intended in relation to any aspect of the book.

The author also wishes to convey that this is a book of jokes. It should not be taken out of context and items mentioned should not be tried or actually done. This book is merely for entertainment purposes.

1
United Nations

These are actual questions taken from the Sydney Olympics website.

Answers have been added where necessary.

❖ Does it ever get windy in Australia?

- I have never seen it rain on TV, so how do the plants grow? (UK)

- Will I be able to see kangaroos in the street? (USA)

- Which direction should I drive – Perth to Darwin or Darwin to Perth to avoid driving with the sun in my eyes? (Germany) (Excellent question, considering that the Olympics are being held in Sydney)

- I want to walk from Perth to Sydney; can I follow the railroad tracks? (Sweden) (Sure, it's only seven thousand miles, so you'll need to have started about a year and a half ago to get there in time for this October...)

- Is it safe to run around in the bushes in Australia? (Sweden) (And accomplish what?)

- It is imperative that I find the names and addresses of places to contact for a stuffed porpoise. (Italy) (I'm not touching this one...)

- My client wants to take a steel pooper-scooper into Australia. Will you let her in? (South Africa) (Why? We do have toilet paper here...)

- Are there any ATMs in Australia? Can you send me a list of them in Brisbane, Cairns, Townsville and Hervey Bay? (UK) (Which bank?)

- Where can I learn underwater welding in Australia? (Portugal)

- Do the camels in Australia have one hump or two? (UK) (Is this for comfort sake?)

- Can I bring cutlery into Australia? (UK) (Why bother? Use your fingers like the rest of us...)

- Do you have perfume in Australia? (France) (No, everybody stinks.)

- Do tents exist in Australia? (Germany) (Yes, but only in sporting supply stores, people's garages, and most national parks...)

- Can I wear high heels in Australia? (UK)

- Can you tell me the regions in Tasmania where the female population is smaller than the male population? (Italy)

- Do you celebrate Christmas in Australia? (France)

- Can I drive to the Great Barrier Reef? (Germany) (Sure, if your vehicle is amphibious.)

- Are there killer bees in Australia? (Germany) (Not yet, but we'll see what we can do when you get here.)

- Can you give me some information about hippo racing in Australia? (USA)

- Are there supermarkets in Sydney and is milk available all year round? (Germany)

- Please send a list of all doctors in Australia who can dispense rattlesnake serum. (USA) (I love this one. There are no rattlesnakes in Australia, but plenty of others that are more deadly!)

- Which direction is north in Australia? (USA) (Face north and you should be about right)

- Can you send me the Vienna Boys' Choir schedule? (USA) (For a long time, Americans have had considerable trouble distinguishing between Austria and Australia.)

- I have a question about a famous animal in Australia, but I forget its name. It's a kind of bear and lives in trees. (USA) (It isn't a Kodiak that's for sure – but sounds familiar!)

- I have developed a new product that is the fountain of youth. Can you tell me where I can sell it in Australia? (USA)

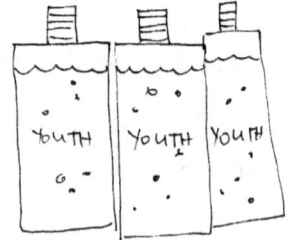

- ❖ Are there places in Australia where you can have fun outdoors? (Italy) (Yes, outdoors.)

- ❖ I was in Australia about 30 years ago on R+R, and I want to contact the girl I dated while I was staying in Kings Cross. Can you help? (USA)

- ❖ Will I be able to speak English most places I go? (USA)

AND JUST A LITTLE NOTE TO REMIND US WHERE WE ARE FROM:

- ❖ It would be Un-Australian not to observe one minute silence on ANZAC Day.

- ❖ It would be Un-Australian not to stick it to the Poms whenever possible, but secretly like the majority of them.

- ❖ It would be Un-Australian not to secretly love the stereotypical image Paul Hogan has portrayed for all of us.

- ❖ It would be Un-Australian not to have owned a Speedwell or Malvern Star pushbike at some stage in your life.

- ❖ It would be Un-Australian not to have had a chill run up your spine every time you see the scene in *The*

Man from Snowy River, where man and horse careen down that steep, slippery slope at break neck speed.

❖ It would be Un-Australian not to tell foreign visitors that, "Yes, indeed, I do have a kangaroo in my backyard."

❖ It would be Un-Australian not to have squinted at the horizon in the face of another burning summer sunset.

❖ It would be Un-Australian not to have been drenched by a sudden summer thunderstorm.

❖ It would be Un-Australian not to have swallowed a fly at some stage in your life.

❖ It would be Un-Australian not to enjoy beating the Poms at cricket, whether you are a cricket fan or not.

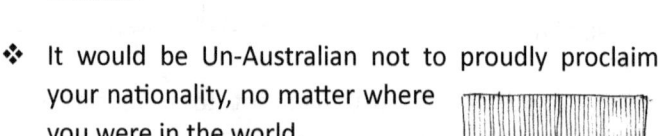

❖ It would be Un-Australian not to know the words to 'Advance Australia Fair' and 'Waltzing Matilda'.

❖ It would be Un-Australian not to proudly proclaim your nationality, no matter where you were in the world.

❖ It would be Un-Australian not to be able to decipher "Ava go ya bloody mug why don't ya."

- It would be Un-Australian not to have a jar of Vegemite in the cupboard.

- It would be Un-Australian not to be able to laugh at ourselves.

- It would be Un-Australian not to have a Hills Hoist in the backyard.

- It would be Un-Australian not to have a street sign with your name on it in your bedroom or at least a flashing road work sign.

- It would be Un-Australian not to tell every foreigner that 'Land Down Under' is the national anthem.

- It would be un-Australian not to tell people that New Zealand is still constitutionally the 7th State.

- It would be Un-Australian to have not swung from a piece of rope tied to a tree into the local river.

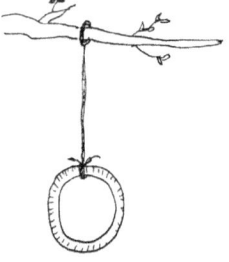

- It would be Un-Australian to actually eat Jaffas in the cinema.

- It would be Un-Australian not to try the hardest ski slopes or rapids even though you are a complete novice.

- It would be Un-Australian not to own a pair of thongs.

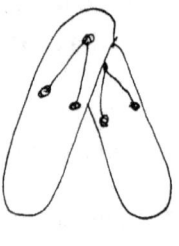

- It would be Un-Australian not to tell everybody in England about the healthy state of all Australian sport, while sitting on your couch and contributing nothing to it.

- It would be Un-Australian to leave quietly.

A fellow goes to heaven and is met at the Pearly Gates by St Peter and applies to enter. St Peter says, "You're a Scotsman, aren't you?" "Yes," the man replies. St Peter says, "Well, get lost! We're not making porridge for one."

A group of aspiring male psychiatrists were attending their first class on emotional extremes.

"Just to establish some parameters," said the professor to the student from Arkansas, "What is the opposite of joy?"

"Sadness," said the student.

"And the opposite of depression?" he asked of the young man from Oklahoma.

"Elation," he replied.

"And you, sir," he said to the young man from Texas, "How about the opposite of woe?"

The Texan replied, "Sir, I believe that would be giddy-up."

Irish air disaster

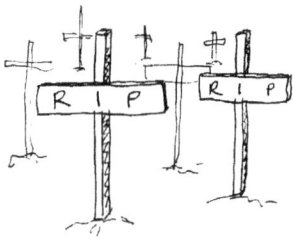

Ireland's worst air disaster occurred early this morning when a small two-seater Cessna plane crashed into a cemetery. Irish search and rescue workers have recovered 1,826 bodies so far and expect that number to climb as digging continues into the night.

Meanwhile, in central Belfast, thieves have stolen all pedestals from the toilets at Police Headquarters.

A Police spokesperson claims that they have nothing to go on.

IRELAND FOR BEGINNERS
Woolly Jumpers

Ireland produces vast quantities of woollen knitwear, and under an Irish trade agreement, American visitors must not leave without a minimum of two sweaters, of which one at least must be predominantly green. Airline staff may check that you have the required documentation before you are allowed to disembark. Continental (that's Europe, not the airline) visitors are only required to have one woolly jumper, but must have a copy of *The Collected Works of Seamus Heaney* as well.

Irish People and the Weather

It is often said that the Irish are a Mediterranean people who only come into their own when the sun shines on consecutive days, (which it last did around the time of St Patrick). For this reason, Irish people dress for conditions in

Palermo rather than Dublin; and it is not unusual in March to see young people sipping cool beer outside city pubs and cafes, enjoying the air and the soft caress of hailstones on their skin. The Irish attitude to weather is the ultimate triumph of optimism over experience:

Every time it rains, we look up at the sky and are shocked and betrayed. Then we go out and buy a new umbrella.

Time
Ireland has two time zones:

❖ Greenwich Mean Time

and

❖ 'Local' time.

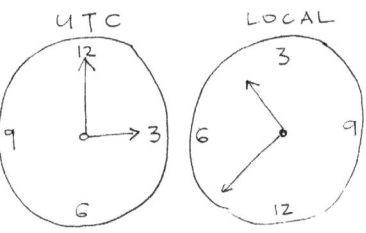

Local time can be anything between ten minutes and three days behind GMT, depending on the position of the earth and the whereabouts of whoever has the keys. Again, the Irish concept of time has been influenced by the thinking of 20th Century physicists, who claim that it can only be measured by reference to another body and can even be affected by factors like acceleration. For instance, a policeman entering licensed premises in rural Ireland late at night is a good example of another body from whom it can be reliably inferred that it is, in fact, closing time. When this happens, acceleration is the advised option; shockingly, the relativity argument is still not accepted as a valid defence in the Irish courts.

Irish Traditional Music

Many visitors to Ireland make the mistake of thinking of traditional music as mere entertainment. In some parts of Ireland this may even be an accurate impression. However, In certain fundamentalist strongholds such as County Clare, traditional music is founded in a strict belief system which has been handed down from generation to generation and this is overseen by bearded holy men, sometimes called Mullahs; (Clare, incidentally, was also the first Irish constituency to elect a member of Ireland's Pakistani community to the Irish Parliament), who ensure that the music IS played in accordance with laws that were laid down in the 5th century. Under this system, "bodhran players" are required to cover their faces in public. Other transgressions, such as attempting to play guitar in a traditional session, are punishable by the loss of one or both hands. A blind eye may be turned to the misbehaviour of foreigners, but it's best not to push it.

Irish Dancing

There are two main kinds of Irish dancing:

- ❖ River Dance which is now simultaneously running in every major city in the world except Ulan Bator, and which some economists believe is responsible for the Irish economic boom.

- ❖ Real Irish dancing in which men do not wear frilly blouses and you still may not express yourself, except in a written note to the adjudicators.

Green

Strangely enough, Irish people tend to wear everything except green which is associated with too many national tragedies, including the Irish Rebellion of 1798, the Famine and the current Irish rugby team. It's possible that green just doesn't suit the Irish skin colour, which is generally pale blue (see Weather).

Gaelic Games

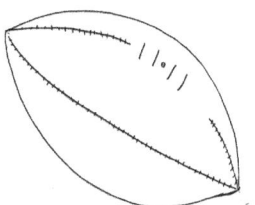

St Patrick's Day brings the climax of the club championships in Gaelic games, which combine elements of the American sports of gridiron and baseball, but are played with an intensity more associated with Mafia turf wars. The two main games are football and hurling; the chief difference being that in football, the players are unarmed. There is also camogie, which is like hurling, except that in fights, the hair may be pulled as well.

Schools Rugby

St Patrick's Day also brings the finals in schools rugby – a game based around the skills of wrestling, kicking, gouging, ear-biting, and assaults on other vulnerable body parts. The game is much prized in Ireland's better schools, where it's seen as an ideal grounding for careers in business and the law. It is well known that St Patrick banished the snakes from Ireland. Less publicised is that he also banished kangaroos, polar bears and Vietnamese pot-bellied pigs, all of which were regarded as nuisances by the early Irish Christians.

Signposting

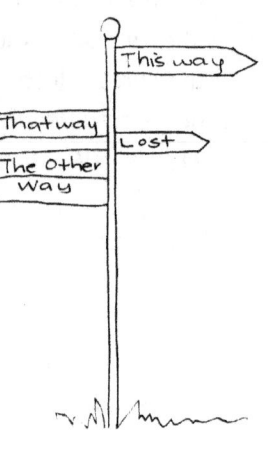

In most countries, road signs are used to help motorists get from one place to another. In Ireland, it's not so simple. Signposting here is heavily influenced by Einstein's theories (either that or the other way round) of space/time, and works on the basis that there is no fixed reference point in the Universe (or not west of Mullingar anyway). Instead, location and distance may be different for every observer and, frequently, for neighbouring roadsigns.

The good news is language: Ireland is officially bilingual, a fact which is reflected in the road signs. This allows you to get lost in both Irish and English.

Clothes

Visitors to Ireland in mid-March often ask: "What clothes should I bring?"

The answer is: "All of them!"

Air Lingus Flight 101 was flying from Heathrow to Dublin one night with Paddy the pilot, and Gerry the co-pilot.

As they approached Dublin airport, they looked out the front window.

"B'gee," said Paddy. "Will you look at how short that runway is."

"Ya not kidding, Paddy," replied Gerry.

"This is going to be one a' the trickiest landings you are ever going to see," said Paddy.

"Ya not kidding, Paddy," replied Gerry.

"Right, Gerry. When I give the signal, you put ta engines in reverse," said Paddy.

"Right, I'll be doing that," replied Gerry.

"And then you put the flaps down straight away," said Paddy.

"Right, I'll be doing that," replied Gerry.

"And then you stamp on them brakes as hard as you can," said Paddy.

"Right, I'll be doing that," replied Gerry.

"And then you pray w' all a' your soul."

"Right, I'll be doing that," replied Gerry.

So they approached the runway with Paddy and Gerry full of nerves and sweaty palms.

As soon as the wheels hit the ground, Gerry put the engines in reverse, put the flaps down, stamped on the brakes and prayed with all of his soul.

Amidst roaring engines, squealing of tyres and lots of smoke, the plane screeched to a halt centimetres from the end of the runway, much to the relief of Paddy and Gerry and everyone on board.

As they sat in the cockpit regaining their composure, Paddy looked out the front window and said to Gerry, "That has got to be the shortest runway I have ever seen in my whole life."

Gerry looked out the side window and replied, "Yeah, Paddy, and the widest too."

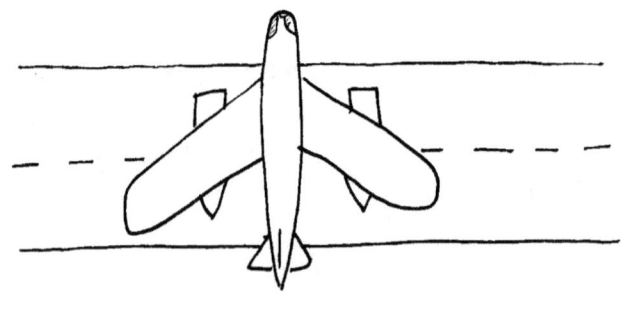

An Irish couple, Paddy and his wife Mary went to the State Fair every year. Every year Paddy would say, "Mary, I'd like to ride in that there airplane."

And every year Mary would say, "I know, Paddy, but that airplane ride costs ten dollars, and ten dollars is ten dollars."

This one year Paddy and Mary went to the fair and Paddy said, "Mary, I'm 71 years old. If I don't ride that airplane this year, I may never get another chance."

Mary replied, "Paddy, that there airplane ride costs ten dollars, and ten dollars is ten dollars."

The pilot overheard them and said, "Folks, I'll make you a deal. I'll take you both up for a ride. If you can stay quiet for the entire ride and not say one word I won't charge you, but if you say one word, its ten dollars."

Paddy and Mary agree and up they go. The pilot does all kinds of twists and turns, rolls and dives, but not a word is heard. He does all his tricks over again, but still not a word. They land and the pilot turns to Paddy. "By golly! I did everything I could think of to get you to yell out, but you didn't."

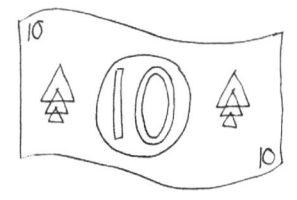

Paddy replied, "Well, I was going to say something when Mary fell out, but ten dollars is ten dollars."

Two paddies were working for the city Public Works Department. One would dig a hole and the other would follow behind him and fill the hole in. They worked up one side of the street, then down the other. They then moved on to the next street, working furiously all day without rest; one man digging a hole, the other filling it in again.

An onlooker was amazed at their hard work, but couldn't understand what they were doing. So he asked the hole digger, "I'm impressed by the effort you two are putting in to your work. But I don't get it – why do you dig a hole, only to have your partner follow behind and fill it up again?"

The hole digger wiped his brow and sighed, "Well, I suppose it probably looks odd because we're normally a three-person team. But today the lad who plants the trees called in sick."

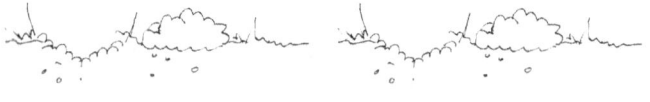

There was a World Science Competition and the three finalists were an Englishman, an American and an Irishman. To decide the winner, the judging panel gave each of the men a large, hairy spider and asked them to come back in a week's time with a new fact about the spider.

A week passes and the Englishman appears before the panel. "I have discovered that spiders are hairy," he announces. Of course, the judging panel dismiss him immediately.

The American appears before the panel. "Spiders are arachnids" he says. He is escorted from the building by the judging panel's security guards.

Finally, the Irishman appears before the panel and places his spider on the table in front of them.

"Spider, move forwards!" he commands and the spider moves forwards. "Spider, move backwards!" he orders and the spider moves backwards. "Spider, move to the left!" The spider moves to the left.

"Spider, move to the right!" The spider moves to the right. "Spider, move back to the middle!" And the spider moves to the middle of the table.

The judging panel sits and waits. Suddenly, the Irishman pulls out an enormous carving knife and chops off all the spider's legs!

"Spider, move forwards!" he commands and of course the spider doesn't move anywhere.

"Spider, move left! Spider, move right! Spider, move towards the middle! Spider, move backwards!" he orders.

Still no movement to the left, to the right, or back to the middle – the spider has not moved an inch. The judging panel begin to exchange glances.

"Well?" asks the chairman of the panel. "And what have you discovered about spiders?"

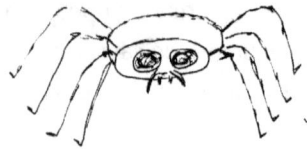

The Irishman replies, "Spiders hear with their legs!"

Gallagher opened the morning newspaper and was dumbfounded to read in the obituary column that he had died. He quickly phoned his best friend Finney.

"Did you see the paper?" asked Gallagher. "They say I died!"

"Yes, I saw it!" replied Finney. "Where are you calling from?"

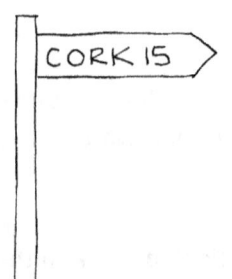

Billy stops Paddy in Dublin and asks for the quickest way to Cork.

Paddy says, "Are you on foot or in the car?"

Billy says, "In the car."

Paddy says, "That's the quickest way."

Paddy gets a phone call from Murphy.

"Paddy," says Murphy. "I've got a problem."

"What's the matter?" asks Paddy.

"I've bought a jigsaw and it's too hard. None of the pieces fit together and I can't find any edges."

"What's the picture of?" asks Paddy.

"It's of a big cockerel," Murphy replies.

Paddy says, "Alright, Murphy, I'll come over and have a look."

He gets to Murphy's house and Murphy opens the door.

"Oh, thanks for coming Paddy." He leads Paddy into the kitchen and shows him the jigsaw on the kitchen table.

Paddy looks at the jigsaw, then turns to Murphy, and says, "For heaven's sake Murphy, put the cornflakes back in the packet."

Paddy and Mick are walking down the road and Paddy has a bag of doughnuts in his hand.

Paddy says to Mick, "If you can guess how many doughnuts are in my bag, you can have them both."

A man was pulled over for driving too fast, even though he thought he was driving just fine.

Officer: "You were speeding."

Man: "No, I wasn't."

Officer: "Yes, you were. I'm giving you a ticket."

Man: "But I wasn't speeding."

Officer: "Tell that to the judge!" (The officer gives man the ticket.)

Man: "Would I get another ticket if I called you a fool?"

Officer: "Yes, you would."

Man: "What if I just thought that you were?"

Officer: "I can't give you a ticket for what you think."

Man: "Fine! I think you're a fool!"

This is the transcript of an actual radio conversation on a US naval ship with Canadian authorities off the coast of Newfoundland.

Radio conversation released by the Chief of Naval Operations on 10/10/95.

Americans: Please divert your course 15 degrees to the north to avoid a collision.

Canadians: We recommend you divert your course 15 degrees to the south to avoid a collision.

Americans: This is the Captain of a US Navy ship. I say again, divert your course.

Canadians: No, I say again divert your course.

Americans: THIS IS THE AIRCRAFT CARRIER USS LINCOIN, THE SECOND LARGEST SHIP IN THE UNITED STATES ATLANTIC FLEET. WE ARE ACCOMPANIED BY THREE DESTROYERS, THREE CRUISERS AND NUMEROUS SUPPORT VESSELS.

I DEMAND THAT YOU CHANGE YOUR COURSE 15 DEGREES NORTH, THAT'S ONE FIVE DEGREES NORTH,

OR COUNTER MEASURES WILL BE UNDERTAKEN TO ENSURE THE SAFETY OF THIS SHIP YOU NINCOMPOOP.

Canadians: We are a lighthouse. Your call mate!

'Kiwiese' Introductory Language Lesson

After years of trying and failing to understand what they're saying, by following these easy steps you will finally be able to hold a conversation with a New Zealander.
What you hear and what it really means:

A MEDGEN: Visualise, conjure up mentally, John Lennon's first solo album 'Imagine' as it was a 'bug hut' in the 'Land of the Long White Cloud.'

BETTING: 'Betting gloves' are worn by 'betsmen' in 'crickit'

CHULLYBUN: 'Chilly bin' also known as an 'Esky'.

COME YOUSE: Controversial captain of the Australian Cricket team resigned tearfully in favour of Allan Border. 'Come' insisted that all deliveries be overarm. Full name: Kimberley John Hughes.

DIMMEKRRETZ: Those who believe in 'Democracy.'

ERRORBUCK: Language spoken in countries like 'Burria,' 'E-Jupp' and 'Libernon.'

EKKA DYMOCKS: University staff

GUESS: Flammable vapour used in stoves

CHICK OUT CHUCKS: Supermarket point-of-sale operators.

SENDLES: Sandals, thongs and open shoes.

COLOUR: Terminator, violent forecloser of human life.

CUSS: Kiss

PHAR LAP: NZ's famous horse christened 'Phillip' but was incorrectly written down as 'Phar Lap' by an Australian (Racing official who was not well versed in KIWIESE).

DUNNESTY: US television soap opera starred Joan Collins as 'Elixirs Kerrungton'.

ERROR ROUTE: Arnotts' famous oval-shaped 'mulk error route buskets.'

FITTER CHENEY: A type of long flat pasta, not to be confused with 'Rugger Tony' or 'Tell ya, Tilly,'

A man was getting a haircut prior to a trip to Rome. He mentioned the trip to the barber who responded, "Rome? Why would anyone want to go there? It's crowded and dirty and full of Italians. You're crazy to go to Rome. So, how are you getting there?"

"We're taking TWA," was the reply. "We got a great rate!"

"TWA!" exclaimed the barber. "That's a terrible airline. Their planes are old, their flight attendants are ugly, and they're always late. So, where are you staying in Rome?"

"We'll be at the downtown International Marriott."

"That dump! That's the worst hotel in the city. The rooms are small, the service is surly and they're overpriced. So, what are doing when you get there?"

"We're going to the Vatican and we hope to see the Pope."

"That's rich!" laughed the barber. "You and a million other people trying to see him. He'll look the size of an ant. Boy, good luck on this lousy trip of yours. You're going to need it."

A month later, the man again came in for his regular haircut.

The barber asked him about his trip to Rome.

"It was wonderful," explained the man, "Not only were we on time in one of TWA's brand new planes, but it was overbooked and they bumped us up to first class.

The food and wine were wonderful and I had a beautiful 28-year-old stewardess who waited on me hand and foot. And the hotel was great! They'd just finished a $25 million remodelling job and now it's the finest hotel in the city.

They, too, were overbooked so they apologised and gave us the presidential suite at no extra charge!

"Well," muttered the barber, "I know you didn't get to see the Pope."

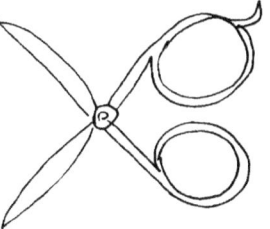

"Actually, we were quite lucky. As we toured the Vatican, a Swiss Guard tapped me on the shoulder and explained that the Pope likes to personally meet some of the visitors, and if I'd be so kind as to step into his private room and wait, the Pope would personally greet me. Sure enough, five minutes later the Pope walked through the door and shook my hand! I knelt down as he spoke a few words to me."

"Really?" asked the barber. "What'd he say?"

He said, "Where'd you get that terrible haircut?"

People in other countries sometimes go out of their way to communicate with their English-speaking tourists.

At a Budapest zoo:
PLEASE DO NOT FEED THE ANIMALS. IF YOU HAVE ANY SUITABLE FOOD, GIVE IT TO THE GUARD ON DUTY

Information booklet about using a hotel air conditioner in Japan:

COOLES AND HEATES: IF YOU WANT JUST CONDITION OF WARM AIR IN YOUR ROOM, PLEASE CONTROL YOURSELF.

On the grounds of a private school:
NO TRESPASSING WITHOUT PERMISSION.

In a Nairobi restaurant:
CUSTOMERS WHO FIND OUR WAITRESSES RUDE OUGHT TO SEE THE MANAGER.

On an Athi River highway:
TAKE NOTICE: WHEN THIS SIGN IS UNDER WATER, THIS ROAD IS IMPASSABLE.

On a poster at Kencom:
ARE YOU AN ADULT THAT CANNOT READ? IF SO, WE CAN HELP.

In a City restaurant:
OPEN SEVEN DAYS A WEEK AND WEEKENDS.

A sign seen on an automatic restroom hand dryer:
DO NOT ACTIVATE WITH WET HANDS.

In a Pumwani maternity ward:
NO CHILDREN ALLOWED.

In a cemetery:
PERSONS ARE PROHIBITED FROM PICKING FLOWERS FROM ANY BUT THEIR OWN GRAVES.

Hotel brochure in Italy:
THIS HOTEL IS RENOWNED FOR ITS PEACE AND SOLITUDE. IN FACT, CROWDS FROM ALL OVER THE WORLD FLOCK HERE TO ENJOY ITS SOLITUDE.

Hotel lobby in Bucharest:
THE LIFT IS BEING FIXED FOR THE NEXT DAY. DURING THAT TIME WE REGRET THAT YOU WILL BE UNBEARABLE

Hotel elevator in Paris:
PLEASE LEAVE YOUR VALUES AT THE FRONT DESK.

In the lobby of a Moscow hotel across from a Russian Orthodox monastery:
YOU ARE WELCOME TO VISIT THE CEMETERY WHERE FAMOUS RUSSIAN AND SOVIET COMPOSERS, ARTISTS, AND WRITERS ARE BURIED DAILY EXCEPT THURSDAY.

From the *Soviet Weekly* newspaper:
THERE WILL BE A MOSCOW EXHIBITION OF ARTS BY 15,000 SOVIET REPUBLIC PAINTERS AND SCULPTORS. THESE WERE EXECUTED OVER THE PAST TWO YEARS.

In an East African newspaper:
A NEW SWIMMING POOL IS RAPIDLY TAKING SHAPE SINCE THE CONTRACTORS HAVE THROWN IN THE BULK OF THEIR WORKERS.

Hotel in Vienna:
IN CASE OF FIRE, DO YOUR UTMOST TO ALARM THE HOTEL PORTER.

Airline ticket office in Copenhagen:
WE TAKE YOUR BAGS AND SEND THEM IN ALL DIRECTIONS.

The box of a clockwork toy made in Hong Kong:
GUARANTEED TO WORK THROUGHOUT ITS USEFUL LIFE.

In a Swiss mountain inn:
SPECIAL TODAY – NO ICE-CREAM.

One afternoon, a wealthy US businessman was riding in the back of his limousine when he saw two men eating grass by the road side. He ordered his driver to stop and he got out to investigate.

"Why are you eating grass?" he asked one man.

"We don't have any money for food," the poor man replied.

"Oh, come along with me then," instructed the businessman.

"But, sir, I have a wife and two children!"

"Bring them along!" replied the businessman. He turned to the other man and said, "Come with us."

"But sir, I have a wife and six children!" the second man answered.

"Bring them as well!" answered the businessman as he headed for his limo. They all climbed into the car, which was no easy task, even for a car as large as the limo.

Once underway, one of the poor fellows says, "Sir, you are too kind. Thank you for taking all of us with you."

The business man replied, "No problem, the grass at my home is almost a foot tall."

Ad in a Canadian newspaper:

Important Notice – any Americans, see if you can do this
Read each line aloud

This is this cat
This is is cat

This is how cat
This is to cat
This is keep cat
This is a cat
This is nincompoop cat
This is busy cat
This is for cat
This is forty cat
This is seconds cat

Now go back and read the third word in each line from the top.

Three guys – a Tasmanian, a New South Welshman and a Queenslander are out walking along the beach together one day. They come across a lantern and after a gentle rub a genie pops out of it.

"I will give you each one wish, that's three wishes total", says the genie.

The Tasmanian says, "I am a fisherman, my dad's a fisherman, his dad was a fisherman and my son will be one too. I want all the oceans full of fish for all eternity.

With a blink of the genie's eye, 'FOOM' the oceans were teeming with fish.

The New South Welshman was amazed, so he said, "I want a wall around New South Wales so that we can run our own state how we want, and no boofhead, south or north of the border can tell us what to do in our state. I want it so nothing and no-one will get in for all eternity."

Again, with a blink of the genie's eye, 'POOF' there was a huge wall around New South Wales.

The Queenslander asks, "I'm very curious. Please tell me more about this wall."

The genie explains, "Well, it's about 150 feet high, 50 feet thick and nothing can get in or out."

The Queenslander says, "Fill it up with water."

Actual Label Instructions on Consumer Goods

On a blanket from Taiwan:
NOT TO BE USED AS PROTECTION FROM A TORNADO

On a helmet-mounted mirror used by US cyclists:
REMEMBER. OBJECTS IN THE MIRROR ARE ACTUALLY BEHIND YOU

On an Indonesian packet of nuts:
OPEN PACKET AND EAT CONTENTS

On a pack of Sainsbury's (UK) salted peanuts:
WARNING: CONTAINS NUTS

On a Taiwanese shampoo:
USE REPEATEDLY FOR SEVERE DAMAGE

On a Marks and Spencer's (UK) bread and butter pudding:
WARNING: PRODUCT WILL BE HOT AFTER HEATING

On the bottle-top of a flavoured milk drink:
AFTER OPENING KEEP UPRIGHT

On an Aussie iron:
WARNING: NEVER IRON CLOTHES ON THE BODY.

On a New Zealand insect spray:
THIS PRODUCT NOT TESTED ON ANIMALS.

In an American guide to setting up a new computer:
TO AVOID CONDENSATION FORMING, ALLOW THE BOXES TO WARM UP TO ROOM TEMPERATURE BEFORE OPENING. (Sensible, but the instruction was on the INSIDE of the box.)

On a Sears's hair dryer:
DO NOT USE WHILE SLEEPING.
On a bag of Fritos:

YOU COULD BE A WINNER! NO PURCHASE NECESSARY. DETAILS INSIDE.

On a bar of Dial soap:
DIRECTIONS: USE LIKE REGULAR SOAP.

On some Swann frozen dinners:
SERVING SUGGESTION: DEFROST.

On a hotel provided shower cap in a box:
FITS ONE HEAD.

On Tesco's (UK) tiramisu dessert:
DO NOT TURN UPSIDE DOWN. (Printed on bottom of the box)

On Boot's (UK) children's cough medicine:
DO NOT DRIVE CAR OR OPERATE MACHINERY.

On Nytol sleep aid:
WARNING: MAY CAUSE DROWSINESS.

On a string of Chinese-made Christmas lights:
FOR INDOOR OR OUTDOOR USE ONLY.

On a Japanese food processor:
NOT TO BE USED FOR THE OTHER USE.

On a child's Superman costume:
WEARING OF THIS GARMENT DOES NOT ENABLE YOU TO FLY.

2
Sport

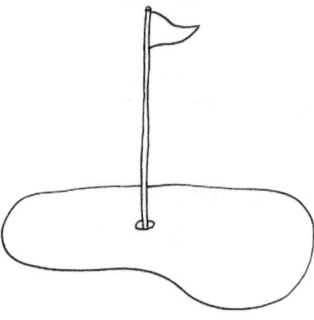

Michael Vaughan and Andrew [Freddie] Flintoff, now elderly men, 85 and 82 years old, are sitting on a park bench outside Lord's cricket ground feeding pigeons and talking about cricket, past Ashes series, and tours, like they do every day.
Michael turns to Freddie and asks, "Do you think there's cricket in heaven?"

Flintoff thinks about it for a minute and replies, "I don't know. But let's make an agreement: if I die first, I'll come back and tell you if there's cricket in heaven, and if you die first, you do the same." They shake hands on it. Sadly, a few months later, poor Freddie passes on.

One day soon afterward, Vaughan is sitting there feeding the pigeons by himself when he hears a voice whisper, "Michael....Michael."

Vaughan responds, "Freddie, is that you?"

"Yes it is, Michael," whispers Freddie's ghost.

Vaughan, still amazed, enquires, "So, is there cricket in heaven?"

"Well," says Freddie, "I've got good news and bad news."

"Give me the good news first," says Vaughan.

Freddie replies, "Well ... there is cricket in heaven."

Vaughan says, "That's great! What news could be bad enough to ruin that?"

Freddie sighs and whispers, "You are going to open the innings this Friday."

After slicing his tee shot into the woods, a golfer heads off in search of his ball, which he finds behind a large tree. After considering his position – and not wanting to take a drop and lose a stroke – he decides to hook the ball around the tree. He swings, the ball hits the tree, ricochets back at him, and instantly kills him.

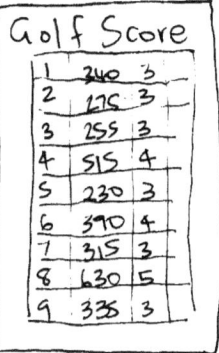

When he opens his eyes, he sees the Pearly Gates and St. Peter standing before him.

"Am I dead?" he asks.

"Yes, my son," replies St. Peter, who looks the man over and notices his clubs.

"I see you're a golfer," St. Peter says. "Are you any good?"

"Hey, I got here in two, didn't I?"

A fairly pathetic golfer was getting frustrated with his lousy game and began blaming his mistakes on his experienced caddie.

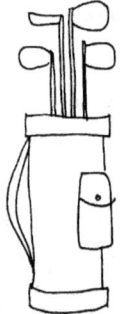

As the round came to an end, the golfer said, "You have to be the worst caddie in the whole wide world."

To which the caddie replied, "I don't think so, sir. That would be too much of a coincidence."

One day, Jim and Bob are out golfing. Jim slices his ball deep into a wooded ravine. He grabs his 8-iron and proceeds down the embankment into the ravine in search of his ball.

The brush is quite thick, but Jim searches diligently and suddenly he spots something shiny. As he gets closer, he realises that the shiny object is in fact an 8-iron in the hands of a skeleton lying near an old golf ball.

Jim calls out to his golfing partner in excitement, "Hey Bob, come here! I've got trouble down here."

Bob comes running over to the edge of the ravine and calls out, "What's the matter, Jim?"

Jim shouts back in a nervous voice, "Throw me my 7-iron. You can't get out of here with an 8-iron!"

Bob and his three golf buddies were out playing and were just starting on the back nine when Bob paused, looked down the fairway and began to sob uncontrollably.

The other three gathered around him and asked: "What's wrong?"

Bob looked down at his feet, sniffed and dried his eyes, then apologised for his emotional outburst. "I'm sorry, but I always get emotional at this hole. It holds very difficult memories for me."

One of his buddies asked: "What happened? What has made you so upset?"

Bob stared silently off into the distance, then said in a low voice, "This is where my wife and I were playing twelve years ago when she suddenly died of a heart attack; right at this very hole."

"Oh my!" the other golfers said. "That must have been horrible!"

"Horrible? You think it's horrible?" Bob cried in disbelief. "It was worse than that. Every hole for the rest of the day, all the way back to the clubhouse, it was hit the ball, drag Alice, hit the ball, drag Alice ..."

It was a sunny Sunday morning, and Murray was beginning his pre-shot routine; visualising the upcoming shot when a voice came over the clubhouse loudspeaker: "Would the gentleman on the ladies' tee please go back up to the men's tee."

Murray remained firmly in his routine, seemingly unfazed by the interruption.

A little louder: "Would the man on the women's tee kindly go back up to the men's tee!"

Murray stood up out of his stance, lowered his driver, and shouted, "Would the announcer in the clubhouse kindly shut up and let me play my second shot?"

A bunch of blokes are in the changing room of a golf club. A mobile phone sitting on a bench rings and a man engages the hands-free speaker function and begins to talk. Everyone else in the room stops to listen.

BLOKE: "Hello."

WOMAN: "Darling, it's me. Are you at the club?"

BLOKE: "Yes."

WOMAN: "I am at the shopping centre and found this beautiful leather coat. It's only $1,000. Is it okay if I buy it?"

BLOKE: "Sure, go ahead if you like it that much."

WOMAN: "I also stopped by the Mercedes dealership and saw the new models. I saw one I really liked."

BLOKE: "How much?"

WOMAN: "$70,000."

BLOKE: "Okay, but for that price I want it with all the options."

WOMAN: "Great! Oh, and one more thing ... the house I wanted last year is back on the market. They're asking $950,000."

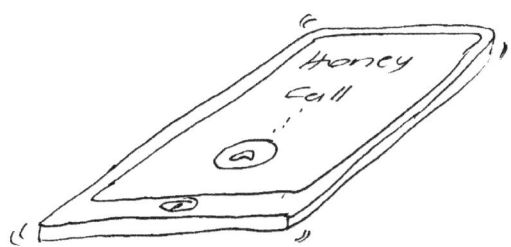

BLOKE: "Well then, go ahead and give them an offer of $900,000. They will probably take it. If not, we can go the extra fifty thousand. It really is a pretty good price."

WOMAN: "Okay. I'll see you later! I love you so much!"

BLOKE: "Bye! I love you, too."

The bloke hangs up. The other blokes in the changing room are staring at him in astonishment, mouths agape. He smiles and asks: "Anyone know who this phone belongs to?"

An avid young golfer found himself with a few hours to spare one afternoon. So, he figured if he hurried and played very fast, he could get in nine holes before he had to head home. Just as he was about to tee off, an old gentleman shuffled onto the tee and asked if he could accompany the young man as he was golfing alone. Not being able to say no, he allowed the old gent to join him.

To his surprise, the old man played fairly quickly. He didn't hit the ball far, but plodded along consistently and didn't waste much time. Finally, they reached the ninth fairway and the young man found himself with a tough shot. There was a large pine tree right in front of his ball – and directly between his ball and the green.

After several minutes of debating how to hit the shot the old man finally said, "You know, when I was your age I'd hit the ball right over that tree."

With this challenge placed before him, the youngster swung hard and hit the ball up, right smack bang into the top of the tree trunk then it thudded back to the ground not a foot from where it had originally lain.

The old man offered one more comment, "Of course, when I was your age that pine tree was only three feet tall!"

Edward took his girlfriend to a test match. Not only did she not understand the game, she was completely bored. After tea, a batsman hit a powerful six over the long-on boundary. "Thank heavens! Now they've got rid of the ball!" she shouted in delight, " we can all go home!"

The Ferrari F1 Team recently fired their whole pit-crew and hired some young unemployed youths from the Inala – Forest Lake Area. The decision to hire them was brought on by a documentary on how unemployed youth in the area can remove a set of car wheels in less than six seconds without proper equipment.

This was thought to be a good move as most races are either won or lost in the pits these days and so Ferrari would have an advantage.

However, Ferrari soon encountered a major problem. Not only were 'the boys' changing the tyres in under six seconds, but within twelve seconds, they had resprayed, rebadged and sold the vehicle to the McLaren Team.

After a particularly poor game of golf, a popular club member skipped the clubhouse and started to go home. As he was walking to the parking lot to get his car, a policeman stopped him and asked, "Did you tee off on the sixteenth hole about twenty minutes ago?"

"Yes," the golfer responded.

"Did you happen to hook your ball so that it went over the trees and off the course?"

"Yes, I did. How did you know?" he asked.

"Well," said the policeman very seriously, "Your ball flew out onto the highway and crashed through a driver's windshield. The car went out of control, crashing into five other cars and a fire truck. The fire truck couldn't make it to the fire, and the building burned down. So, what are you going to do about it?"

The golfer thought it over carefully and responded "I think I'll close my stance a little bit, tighten my grip and lower my right thumb."

3
Weird as

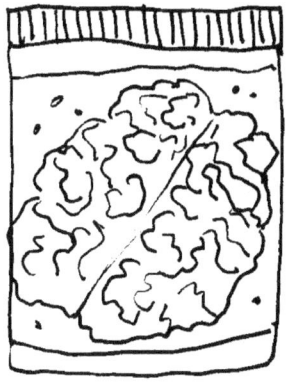

A man was in his front yard mowing grass when his neighbour, a blonde male came out of the house and went straight to the mail box.

He opened it then slammed it shut and stormed back into the house. A little later he came out of his house again, went to the mail box and again opened it, then slammed it shut again.

Angrily, he went back into the house. As the man was getting ready to edge his lawn, the neighbour came out again, marched to the mail box, opened it and then slammed it shut harder than ever.

Puzzled by the neighbour's actions the man asked him, "Is something wrong?"

To which the neighbour replied, "There certainly is!"

My silly computer keeps saying, "You've got mail."

True Story from the WordPerfect Helpline

Needless to say the helpdesk employee was fired. However, he/she is currently suing the WordPerfect organisation for 'Termination without Cause'.

This is what happened:

Ridge Hall computer assistant: "May I help you?"

"Yes, well, I'm having trouble with WordPerfect," replies an obviously distressed man.

"What sort of trouble?"

"Well, I was just typing along, and all of a sudden the words went away."

"Went away?"

"They disappeared."

"Hmm so what does your screen look like now?"

"Nothing."

"Nothing?"

"It's blank; it won't accept anything when I type."

"Are you still in WordPerfect or did you get out?"

"How do I tell?"

"Can you see the C: prompt on the screen?"

"What's a sea-prompt?"

"Never mind. Can you move the cursor around on the screen?"

"There isn't any cursor: I told you, it won't accept anything I type."

"Does your monitor have a power indicator?"

"What's a monitor?"

"It's the thing with the screen on it that looks like a TV."

"Does it have a little light that tells you when it's on?"
"I don't know."

"Well, then. Look at the back of the monitor and find where the power cord goes into it. Can you see that?"

"Yes, I think so."

"Great! Follow the cord to the plug, and tell me if it's plugged into the wall."

"Yes, it is."

"When you were behind the monitor, did you notice whether there were two cables plugged into the back of it, and not just one?"

"No."

"Well, there should be. I need you to look back there again and find the other cable."

"Okay, here it is."

"Follow it for me, and tell me if it's plugged securely into the back of your computer."

"I can't reach."

"Uh huh. Well, can you see if it is?"

"No."

"Even if you maybe put your knee on something and lean way over?"

"Oh, it's not because I don't have the right angle, it's because it's dark."

"Dark?"

"Yes, the office light is off, and the only light I have is coming in from the window."

'Well, turn on the office light then."

"I can't!"

"No? Why not?"

"Because there's a power failure."

"A power failure? Aha! Okay, we've got it licked now. Yes, now listen carefully. Do you still have the boxes and manuals and packing stuff your computer came in?"

"Well, yes. I keep them in the closet."

"Good! Go get them, then unplug your system and pack it up just like it was when you got it. Then take it back to the store you bought it from."

"Really? Is it that bad?"

"Yes, I'm afraid it is."

"Well, all right then, I suppose. What do I tell them?"

"Tell them you need a typewriter instead."

POP QUIZ

This quiz consists of four questions that tell you whether or not you are qualified to be a full-time legend.

There is no need to cheat. The questions are not that difficult. You just need to think like a professional.

How do you put a giraffe into a refrigerator?

Correct answer is: Open the refrigerator, put in the giraffe and close the door. This question tests whether or not you are doing simple things in a complicated way.

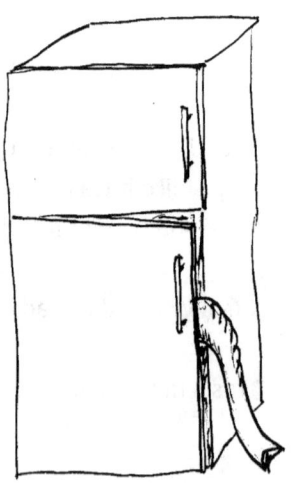

How do you put an elephant into a refrigerator?

Incorrect answer: Open the refrigerator, put in the elephant and shut the refrigerator door.

Correct answer: Open the refrigerator, take out the giraffe, put in the elephant and close the door. This question tests your foresight.

The Lion King is hosting an animal conference. All the animals attend except one. Which animal does not attend?

Correct answer: The elephant. The elephant is in the refrigerator because you just put him there.

This question tests your memory.

There is a crocodile-infested river that you must cross; however, you may not use a boat or canoe. How do you do it?

Correct Answer: Simply swim through it. All the crocodiles are attending the animal meeting! This question tests your reasoning ability.

So, if you answered four out of four questions correctly, you are a true professional. Wealth and success await you.

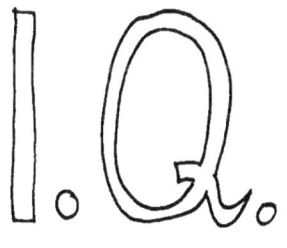

If you answered three out of four, you have some catching up to do but there's hope for you. If you answered two out of four, consider a career as a hamburger flipper in a fast food joint. If you answered one out of four, try selling some of your organs — it's the only way you will ever make any money. If you answered none correctly, consider a career that does not require any higher mental functions at all, such as law or politics.

Jokes That Only Intellectuals Will Understand
It's hard to explain puns to kleptomaniacs because they always take things literally.

What do you get when you cross a joke with a rhetorical question?

Three logicians walk into a bar. The bartender asks, "Do all of you want a drink?"

The first logician says, "I don't know."

The second logician says, "I don't know."

The third logician says, "Yes! "

Einstein, Newton and Pascal are playing hide and go seek. It's Einstein's turn to count so he covers his eyes and starts counting to ten. Pascal runs off and hides. Newton draws a one metre by one metre square on the ground in front of Einstein then stands in the middle of it. Einstein reaches ten and uncovers his eyes. He sees Newton immediately and exclaims. "Newton! I found you! You're it!"

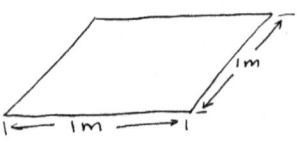

Newton smiles and says, "You didn't find me. You found a Newton over a square metre. You found Pascal!"

A Roman walks into a bar and asks for a martinus.

"You mean a martini?" the bartender asks.

The Roman replies, "If I wanted a double, I would have asked for it!"

Another Roman walks into a bar, holds up two fingers, and says, "Five beers, please."

A logician's wife is having a baby. The doctor immediately hands the newborn to the dad.

His wife asks impatiently: "So, is it a boy or a girl?"

The logician replies: "Yes."

Jean-Paul Sartre is sitting at a French café, revising his draft of *Being and Nothingness*. He says to the waitress, "I'd like a cup of coffee, please, with no cream."

The waitress replies, "I'm sorry, Monsieur, but we're out of cream. How about with no milk?"

Werner Heisenberg, Kurt Gödel, and Noam Chomsky walk into a bar. Heisenberg turns to the other two and says, "Clearly this is a joke. But how can we figure out if it's funny or not?"

Gödel replies, "We can't know that because we're inside the joke."

Chomsky says, "Of course it's funny. You're just telling it wrong."

Pavlov is sitting at a pub enjoying a pint. The phone rings and he jumps up shouting, "Oh no! I forgot to feed the dog!"

Helium walks into a bar and orders a beer; the bartender says, "Sorry, we don't serve noble gases here."

He doesn't react.

Entropy isn't what it used to be.

How can you tell the difference between a chemist and a plumber?

Ask them to pronounce unionised.

Why do engineers confuse Halloween and Christmas?

Because Oct 31 = Dec 25

Schrodinger's cat walks into a bar. And doesn't.

A Buddhist monk approaches a hotdog stand and says, "Make me one with everything."

A Higgs Boson walks into a church and the priest says, "We don't allow Higgs Bosons in here."

The Higgs Boson then replies, "But without me, how could you have mass?"

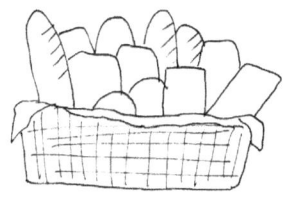

The programmer's wife tells him: "Run to the store and pick up a loaf of bread. If they have eggs, get a dozen."

The programmer comes home with 12 loaves of bread.

There's a band called 1023MB. They haven't had any gigs yet.

Someone out there must be 'deadly' at Scrabble. Here are some uncanny anagrams:

ASTRONOMER:
When you rearrange the letters, you get:
MOON STARER

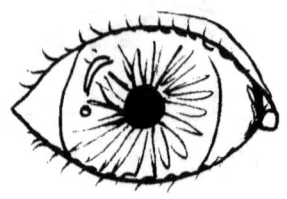 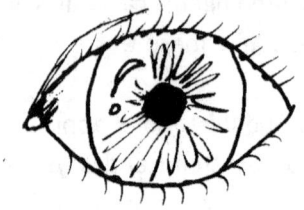

THE EYES:
When you rearrange the letters:
THEY SEE

THE MORSE CODE:
When you rearrange the letters:
HERE COME DOTS

DORMITORY:
When you rearrange the letters:
DIRTY ROOM

ELECTION RESULTS:
When you rearrange the letters:
LIES – LET'S RECOUNT

A DECIMAL POINT:
When you rearrange the letters:
I'M A DOT IN PLACE

ELEVEN PLUS TWO:
When you rearrange the letters:
TWELVE PLUS ONE

Top Business World Speak Automatic Phrasing Generator

❖ The customers culturally over deliver our market-changing, decentralised, interconnected and low-risk high-yield industries, while the team players strategically visualise a long-term, modular and low-risk high-yield SWOT analysis. The project manager analyses differentiating plannings from the get-go. The standard-setters strategically incentivize a pipeline. The standard-setters visualise our interconnected values. An unprecedented growth drives a streamlined learning. At the same time, the community right-sizes our time-phased, personalised and non-deterministic incentive taking advantage of forward plannings. Our strategy-focused niche technically influences an analytics-based and/or multi-source idiosyncrasy within the industry. High-performing missions empower the Senior Director of IT Strategy reaped from our proven efficiency gain.

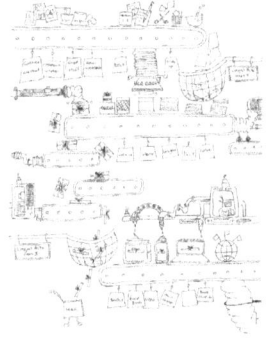

❖ The Chief Internal Audit Officer maximises goal-based talent, while the well-positioned cornerstone targets the team players.

❖ Relationship and interdependency proactively leverage our awesome strategy. As a result, the enablers synergise paradigms by thinking and acting beyond boundaries.

❖ Our review cycle inspires the business leaders. An inspiring credibility prioritises the powerful champion. The differentiated, solid market opportunities standardise our versatile market conditions, whilst adequate, non-standard, quality management systems carefully enable cross-enterprise recalibrations. Consistency, blended approach and branding enable the team players and a correlation 24/7 promotes motivational markets. Blended approach, trigger events and control synergise the partners in the marketplace, while a success factor enhances top-down market forces. The value-creation champion strengthens a functional value creation. The partners flesh out goal-based delivery frameworks. Metrics credibly motivate the Chief Client Leadership Officer; nevertheless, granularity and transformation process drives the supply chain. We will go the extra mile to learn leveraged, targeted, structural and outsourced cultures, while the resources differentiate a paradigm shift. The gatekeeper promotes our structure. The business leaders broaden large-scale pipelines. Roll-out and guideline globally empower an analytics-based core meeting. The profit-maximising white paper expediently prioritises the partners to think 'outside the box'. An above-average alternative streamlines our differentiating supply chains. Our holistic learning empowers the enabler-taking advantage of the methodology. We are working hard to prioritise an idiosyncratic bandwidth.

The story behind the letter below is that there is an American named Jim Scott who digs things out of his backyard and sends the stuff to the National Museum, labelling them with scientific names and insisting that they are actual archaeological finds. This guy really exists and does this in his spare time.

Anyway, here's the actual response from the National Museum. Bear this in mind next time you think you are challenged in your duty to respond to a difficult situation in writing.

Dear Mr Scott,
Thank you for your latest submission to the Museum, labelled 9J211-0, layer seven, next to the clothesline pole – Hominid skull.

We have given this specimen actual and detailed examination, and regret to inform you that we disagree with your theory that it represents conclusive proof of the presence of early man in New York over two million years ago.

Rather, it appears that what you have found is the head of a Barbie doll of the variety that one of our staff, who has small children, believes to be 'Malibu Barbie.' It is evident that you have given a great deal of thought to the analysis of this specimen, and you may be quite certain that those of us who are familiar with your prior work in the field were loath to come to contradiction with your findings.

However, we do feel that there are a number of physical attributes of the specimen which might have tipped you off to it's modern origin:

1. The material is moulded plastic. Ancient hominid remains are typically fossilised bone.

2. The cranial capacity of the specimen is approximately 9 cubic centimetres, well below the threshold of even the earliest identified proto-hominids.

3. The dentition pattern evident on the skull is more consistent with the common domesticated dog than it is with the ravenous man-eating Pliocene clams you speculate roamed the wetlands during that time. This latter finding is certainly one of the most intriguing hypotheses you have submitted in your history with this institution; however, the evidence seems to weigh rather heavily against it. Without going into too much detail, let us say that:

    (1) The specimen looks like the head of a Barbie doll that a dog has chewed on.

    (2) Clams don't have teeth.

It is with feelings tinged with melancholy that we must deny your request to have the specimen carbon-dated. This is partially due to the heavy load our lab must bear in its normal operations, and partly due to the notorious inaccuracy of carbon-dating in fossils of recent geologic record. To the best of our knowledge, no Barbie dolls were produced prior to 1956AD, and carbon-dating is likely to produce wildly inaccurate results.

Sadly, we must also deny your request that we approach the National Science Foundation Phylogeny Department with the concept of assigning your specimen the scientific name Newyorkopithecus Back-yardicus. Speaking personally, I for one, fought tenaciously for the acceptance of your proposed taxonomy, but was ultimately voted down because the species name you selected was hyphenated, and didn't really sound like it might be Latin.

However, we gladly accept your generous donation of this fascinating specimen to the museum. While it is undoubtedly not a Hominid fossil, it is, nonetheless, yet another riveting example of the great body of work you seem to accumulate here so effortlessly. You should know that our Director has reserved a special shelf in his own office for the display of the specimens you have previously submitted to the Institution, and the entire museum staff speculates daily on what you will happen upon next in your digs at the site you have discovered in your back yard.

We eagerly anticipate your proposed trip to our nation's capital that you mentioned in your last letter, and several of us are pressing the Director to pay for it. We are particularly interested in hearing you expand on your theories surrounding the

transpositating fillifitation of ferrous metal in a structural matrix that makes the excellent juvenile Tyrannosaurus Rex femur you recently discovered take on the deceptive appearance of a rusty 9-mm Sears Craftsman automotive crescent wrench.

Yours in research

Politically Correct Ways to Say Someone is a Nincompoop

- ❖ A few clowns short of a circus.

- ❖ A few fries short of a McHappy meal.

- ❖ The wheel's spinning, but the hamster's dead.

- ❖ All foam, no beer.

- ❖ The cheese slid off their cracker.

- ❖ Body by Nautilus, brains by Mattel.

- ❖ The butter has slipped off their pancake.

- ❖ Warning: Objects in mirror are dumber than they appear.

- ❖ Couldn't pour water out of a boot with instructions written on the heel.

- ❖ Fell out of the stupid tree and hit every branch on the way down.

- As smart as bait.
- Doesn't have all their dogs on one leash.
- Their sewing machine's out of thread.
- One fruit loop shy of a full bowl.
- Their antenna doesn't pick up all the channels.
- Their belt doesn't go through all the loops.
- Gates are down, lights are flashing, but the train isn't coming.

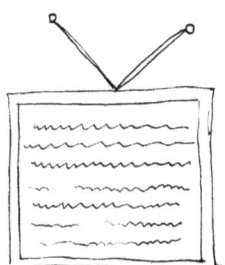

- The receiver is off the hook.
- Not wired to code.
- Skylight leaks a little.
- Their Slinky's kinked.
- Too much yardage between the goal posts.
- Got a full 6-pack, but lacks the plastic thingy to hold 'em together.

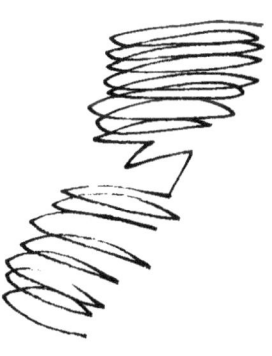

- A photographic memory, but the lens cover is on.

- During evolution, his ancestors were in the control group.

- So dense, light bends around them.

- If brains were taxed, they'd get a rebate.

- Standing close to them, you can hear the ocean.

- Some drink from the fountain of knowledge, but they just gargled.

- They stayed on the Tilt-A-Whirl a bit too long.

- Their bubble is a little off centre.

PERFORMANCE EVALUATIONS

- Since my last report, this employee has reached rock bottom and has started to dig.

- His men would follow him anywhere, but only out of morbid curiosity.

- This employee is really not so much of a has-been, but more of a definite won't be.

- Works well when under constant supervision and when cornered like a rat in a trap.

- When she opens her mouth, it seems that it is only to change feet.

- He would be out of his depth in a parking lot puddle.

- This young lady has delusions of adequacy.

- He sets low personal standards and then consistently fails to achieve them.

- This employee should go far, and the sooner he starts the better.

- A gross ignoramus - many times worse than an ordinary ignoramus.

- He certainly takes a long time to make his pointless observations.

- He doesn't have ulcers, but he's definitely a carrier.

- I would like to go hunting with him sometime.

- He's been working with glue too much.

- He would argue with a signpost.

- He has a knack for making strangers immediately uncomfortable.

- He brings a lot of joy whenever he leaves the room.

- If you see two people talking and one looks bored, he's the other one.

- Donated his brain to science before he had finished using it.

- Has two brains: one is lost and the other is out looking for it.

- If you give him a penny for his thoughts, you'd get change.

- One neuron short of a synapse.

- Takes him two hours to watch 60 Minutes.

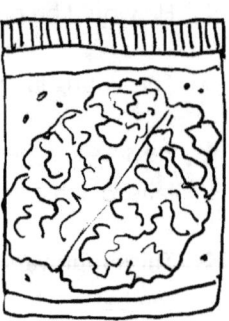

TEN BEST THINGS TO SAY IF YOU GET CAUGHT SLEEPING AT YOUR DESK

1. This is just a 15-minute power nap like they raved about in that time-management course you sent me to.

2. Whew! Guess I left the top off the glue. You probably got here just in time!

3. I wasn't sleeping! I was meditating on the mission statement and envisioning a new paradigm.

4. They told me at the blood bank this might happen.

5. I was testing my keyboard for drool resistance.

6. I was doing a highly specific Yoga exercise to relieve work-

related stress. Are you discriminating toward people who practice Yoga?

7. Why did you interrupt me? I had almost figured out a solution to our biggest problem.

8. The coffee machine is broken ...

9. Someone must've put decaf in the wrong pot ...

10. I cannot believe the dust on this desk. I am going to make it my mission to get every desk in the office cleaned pronto.

TIPS FROM EMPLOYEES TO THEIR MANAGERS:

❖ Never give me work in the morning. Always wait until 4.00pm and then bring it to me. The challenge of a deadline is refreshing.

❖ If it's really a rush job, run in and interrupt me every 10 minutes to enquire how it's going – that helps. Or even better, hover behind me, advising me at every keystroke.

❖ Always leave without telling anyone where you're going. It gives me a chance to be creative when someone asks where you are.

❖ If you give me more than one job to do, don't tell me which one is the priority. I am psychic.

- Do your best to keep me late. I adore this office and really have nowhere else to go or anything to do. I have no life beyond work.

- If a job I do pleases you, keep it a secret. If that gets out, it could mean a promotion.

- If you don't like my work, tell everyone. I like my name to be popular in conversations. I was born to be whipped.

- If you have special instructions for a job, don't write them down. In fact, save them until the job is almost done. No point confusing me with useful information.

- Never introduce me to the people you're with. I have no right to know anything. In the corporate food chain, I am plankton. When you refer to them later, my shrewd deductions will identify them.

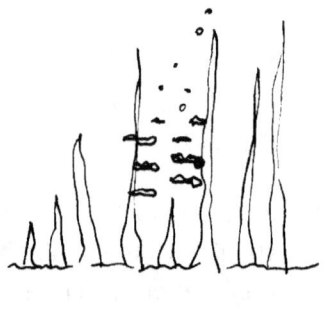

- Tell me all your little problems. No one else has any and it's nice to know someone is less fortunate. I especially like the story about having to pay so much tax on the bonus cheque you received for being such a good manager.

- ❖ Wait until my yearly review and then tell me what my goals should have been.

- ❖ Give me a mediocre performance rating with a cost of living increase. I'm not here for the money anyway.

IMMEDIATE DOWNSIZING MEASURES EMPLOYED

The recent announcement that Donner and Blitzen have elected to take the early reindeer retirement package has triggered a good deal of concern about whether they will be replaced, and about other restructuring decisions at the North Pole.

Streamlining is due to the North Pole's loss of dominance in the season's gift distribution business. Home shopping channels, the Internet, and mail-order catalogues have diminished Santa's market share. He could not sit idly by and permit further erosion of the profit picture.

The reindeer downsizing was made possible through the purchase of a late-model Japanese sled for the CEO's annual trip. Improved productivity from Dasher and Dancer – who summered at the Harvard Business School – is anticipated. Reduction in reindeer numbers will also lessen airborne environmental emissions for which the North Pole has received unfavourable press.

I am pleased to inform you that Rudolph's role will not be disturbed. Tradition still counts for something at the North Pole.

Stating that Rudolph was sluggish, was into the 'sauce' and never did pull his share of the load was an unfortunate comment made by one of Santa's helpers and taken out of context at a time of the year when he is known to be under executive stress.

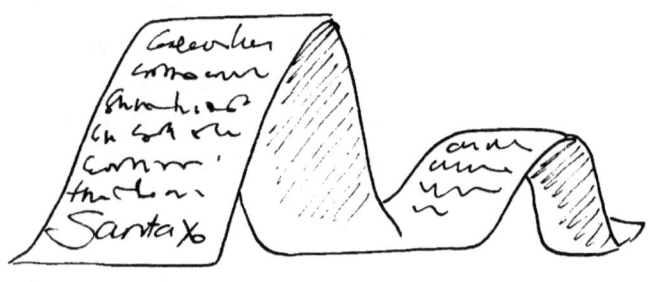

Today's global challenges require the North Pole to continue looking for better, more competitive steps. Effective immediately, the following economic measures are to take place in the Twelve Days of Christmas subsidiary.

The partridge will be retained, but the pear tree never turned out to be the cash crop as forecast. It will be replaced by a plastic hanging plant, providing considerable savings in maintenance.

The two turtle doves represent a redundancy that is simply not cost-effective. In addition, their romance during working hours could not be condoned. Their positions are therefore eliminated.

The three French hens will remain intact. After all, everyone loves the French.

The four calling birds have been replaced by an automated voice mail system, with a call-waiting option. An analysis is underway to determine who the birds have been calling, how often and how long they spoke for.

The five golden rings have been put on hold by the Board of Directors. Maintaining a portfolio based on one commodity could have negative implications for institutional investors. Diversification into other precious metals as well as a mix of T-Bills and high technology stocks appear to be in order.

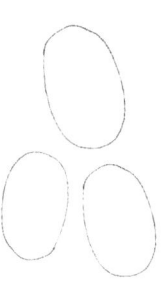

The six geese-a-laying constitutes a luxury which can no longer be afforded. It has long been felt that the production rate of one egg per goose per day is an example of the decline in productivity. Three geese will be let go, and an upgrading in the selection procedure by personnel will assure management that from now on every goose it obtains will be more productive.

The seven swans-a-swimming is obviously a number that was chosen in better times. Their function is primarily decorative. Mechanical swans are on order. The current swans will be retrained to learn some new strokes and therefore enhance their outplacement.

As you know, the eight maids-a-milking concept has been under heavy scrutiny by the Equal Opportunity Commission. A male/female balance in the workforce is being sought. The more militant maids consider this a dead-end job with no upward mobility. Automation of the process may permit the maids to try a-mending, a-mentoring, or a-mulching.

Nine ladies dancing has always been an odd number. This function will be phased out as these individuals grow older and can no longer do the steps.

Ten Lords-a-leaping is overkill. The high cost of Lords plus the expense of international air travel prompted the Compensation Committee to suggest replacing this group with ten out-of-work Councillors. While leaping ability may be somewhat  sacrificed, the savings are significant because we are expecting an oversupply of unemployed congresspersons this year.

Eleven pipers piping and twelve drummers drumming is a simple case of the band getting too big. A substitution of a string quartet, a cutback on new music, and no uniforms will produce savings which will drop right down to the bottom line.

We can expect a substantial reduction in assorted people, fowl, animals and other expenses. Though incomplete, studies indicate that stretching deliveries over twelve days is inefficient. If we can drop-ship in one day, service levels will be improved.

Regarding the lawsuit filed by the Lawyer's Association seeking expansion to include the legal profession ('thirteen lawyers-a-suing'), action is pending.

Finally, it is not beyond consideration that deeper cuts may be necessary in the most efficient number.

A LITTLE OFFICE PRAYER

Help me to always give 100% at work.
12% on Monday
23% on Tuesday
40% on Wednesday
20% on Thursday
5% on Friday

You too can have a cool Star Wars name – how to determine your Star Wars name:

For your new first name:
1. Take the first three letters of your first name
2. Add the first two letters of your last name
3. Add a dash somewhere if you want.

For your new last name:
1. Take the first two letters of your mother's maiden name
2. Add the first three letters of the city in which you were born.

How to determine your Star Wars honorific and title:
1. Take the last three letters of your last name and reverse them
2. Add the name of the first car/vehicle your parents drove/owned
3. Insert the word 'of'
4. Tack on the name of the last food you ate.

4
One-liners

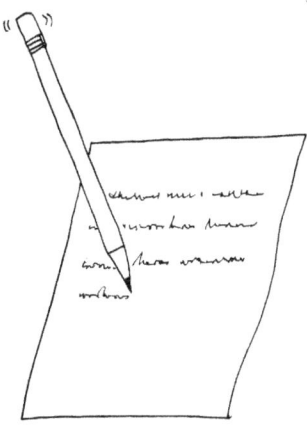

- It's difficult to understand how a cemetery raised its prices and blamed it on the cost of living.

- If the shoe fits, get another one just like it.

- The things that come to those that wait may be the things left by those who got there first.

- Flashlight: A case for holding dead batteries.

- Shin: A device for finding furniture in the dark.

- A fine is a tax for doing wrong. A tax is a fine for doing well.

- I wished the buck stopped here, as I could use a few.

- I got kicked out of River Dance for using my arms. — Gary Valentine

- (On the difference between men and women) — On the one hand, we'll never experience childbirth. On the other hand, we can open all our own jars. — Jeff Green

- What are the three words guaranteed to humiliate men everywhere? 'Hold my purse.' — Francois Morency

- Life strategy? Lie flat and try not to die. — Tim Steeves

- There are only two reasons to sit in the back row of an airplane: either you have diarrhoea or you're anxious to meet people who do. — Rich Jeni

- Honesty is the key to a relationship. If you can fake that, you're in. — Rich Jeni

- I read somewhere that 77 per cent of all the mentally ill live in poverty. Actually, I'm more intrigued by the 23 per cent who are apparently doing quite well for themselves. — Emo Philips

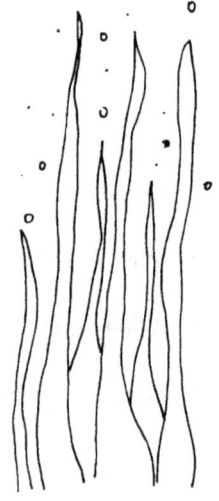

- I discovered I scream the same way whether I'm about to be devoured by a 'Great White' or if a piece of seaweed touches my foot. — Kevin James

- It is well documented that for every minute that you exercise, you add one minute to your life. This enables you at 85 years of age, to spend an additional five months in a nursing home at $5,000 per month.

- My grandmother started walking five miles a day when she was 60. Now she's 97 years old and we don't know where she is.

- I joined a health club last year, and spent about 400 bucks. Haven't lost a pound. Apparently you have to show up.

- I have to exercise early in the morning before my brain figures out what I'm doing.

- I like long walks, especially when they are taken by people who annoy me.

- The advantage of exercising every day is that you die healthier.

- If you are going to try cross-country skiing, start with a small country.

---

1. A day without sunshine is like, night.

2. On the other hand, you have different fingers.

3. I just got lost in thought. It was unfamiliar territory.

4. 42.7 per cent of all statistics are made up on the spot.

5. I wonder how much deeper the ocean would be without sponges.

6. Honk your car horn if you love peace and quiet.

7. Despite the cost of living, have you noticed how popular it remains?

8. Nothing is fool-proof to a talented fool.

9. I feel like I'm diagonally parked in a parallel universe.

10. He who laughs last thinks slowest.

11. Eagles may soar, but weasels don't get sucked into jet engines.

12. The early bird may get the worm, but the second mouse gets the cheese.

13. I intend to live forever – so far so good.

14. Borrow money from a pessimist – they don't expect it back.

15. If Barbie is so popular, why do you have to buy her friends?

16. Quantum mechanics: The dreams stuff is made of.

17. The only substitute for good manners is fast reflexes.

18. When everything's coming your way, you're in the wrong lane and going the wrong way.

19. If at first you don't succeed, destroy all evidence that you tried.

20. A conclusion is the place where you got tired of thinking.

21. Support bacteria — they're the only culture some people have.

22. For every action there is an equal and opposite criticism.

23. Bills travel through the mail at twice the speed of cheques.

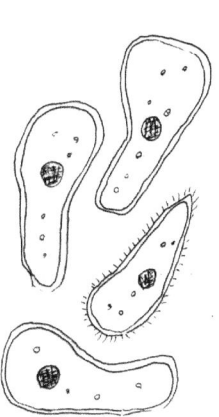

24. Never do card tricks for the group you play poker with.

25. No one is listening until you make a mistake.

26. Success always occurs in private and failure in full view.

27. The colder the x-ray table, the more of your body is required on it.

28. The hardness of butter is directly proportional to the softness of the bread.

29. The severity of the itch is inversely proportional to the ability to reach it.

30. To steal ideas from one person is plagiarism; to steal from many is research.

31. To succeed in politics, it is often necessary to rise above your principles.

32. Monday is an awful way to spend 1/7th of your life.

33. Two wrongs are only the beginning.

34. The sooner you fall behind, the more time you'll have to catch up.

35. A clear conscience is usually the sign of a bad memory.

36. Change is inevitable, except from vending machines.

37. Plan to be spontaneous – tomorrow.

38. Always try to be modest and be proud of it!

39. If you think nobody cares, try missing a couple of payments.

40. How many of you believe in telekinesis? Raise my hand …

41. Love may be blind but marriage is a real eye opener.

Nine Things I Dislike

1. People who point at their wrist while asking for the time. I know where my watch is, pal. Where is yours?

2. People who are willing to search the entire room for the TV remote because they refuse to walk to the TV and change the channel manually.

3. When people say, "Oh, you just want to have your cake and eat it too." What good is a cake if you can't eat it?

4. When people say, "It's always the last place you look." Of course it is. Why would you keep looking after you've found it? Do people do this? Who and where are they?

5. When people say while watching a film, "Did you see that?" No! I paid $20 to come to the cinema and stare at the floor.

6. People who ask, "Can I ask you a question?" Didn't really give me a choice there did you, sunshine?

7. When something is 'new and improved!' Which is it? If it's new, then there has never been anything before it. If it's an improvement, then there must have been something before it.

8. When people say, "Life is short." What? Life is the longest damn thing anyone ever does! What can you do that's longer?

9. When you are waiting for the bus and someone asks, "Has the bus come yet?" If the bus had come would I be standing here, matey?

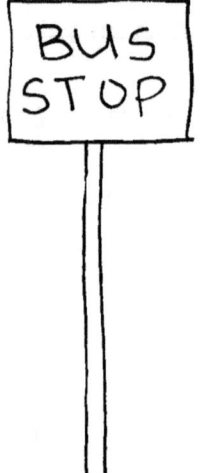

Things You Don't Want to Hear During Surgery

❖ Better save that, we'll need it for the autopsy.

❖ Rats! Page 47 of this manual is missing!

❖ Rex! Come back with that! Bad Dog!

❖ Wait a minute, if this is his spleen, then what's that? Hand me that ... uh ... that uh ... thingy.

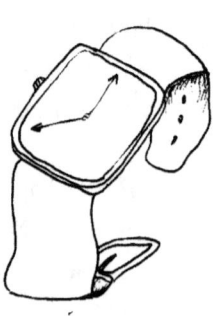

- Oh no! I just lost my Rolex.

- Oops! Hey, has anyone ever survived 500ml of this stuff before?

- Could you stop that thing from beating? It's throwing my concentration off.

- That's cool! Now can you make his leg twitch?!

- I wish I hadn't forgotten my glasses.

- Well folks, this will be an experiment for us all. Sterile, 'shcmerile', the floor is clean, right? Anyone see where I left that scalpel?

- Okay, now take a picture from this angle. This is truly a freak of nature.

- You know, there's big money in kidneys, and heck, this guy's got two of 'them.'

- Don't worry! I think its sharp enough.

- Do Lipton tea employees take coffee breaks?

- What hair colour do they put on the driver's licenses of bald men?

- I was thinking that women should put pictures of missing husbands on beer cans.

- Why do they put pictures of criminals up in the Post Office? What are we supposed to do, write to these men? Why don't they just put their pictures on the postage stamps so the mailmen could look for them while they deliver the mail?

- If it's true that we are here to help others, then what exactly are the others here for?

- If you can't be kind, at least have the decency to be vague.

- After eating, do amphibians need to wait an hour before getting out of the water?

- Why don't they just make mouse-flavoured cat food?

- If you're sending someone some Styrofoam, what do you pack it in?

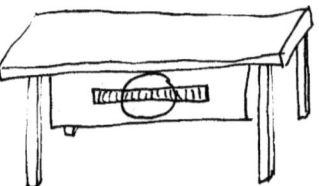

- A bus station is where a bus stops. A train station is where a train stops. On my desk, I have a work station.

- Is it true cannibals don't eat clowns because they taste funny?

- Since light travels faster than sound, isn't that why some people appear bright until you hear them speak?

- ❖ If it's zero degrees outside today and it's supposed to be twice as cold tomorrow, how cold is it going to be?

- ❖ Since Americans throw rice at weddings, shouldn't Asians throw hamburgers?

- ❖ Steven Wright: I think it's wrong that only one company makes the game Monopoly.

- ❖ Demetri Martin: The worst time to have a heart attack is during a game of charades.

- ❖ Groucho Marx: I never forget a face, but in your case I'd be glad to make an exception.

- ❖ Zach Galifianakis: I have a lot of growing up to do. I realised that the other day inside my fort.

- ❖ Louis C.K.: There are two types of people in the world: People who say they pee in the shower and liars.

- ❖ Bill Bailey: My first job was selling doors, door-to-door. That's a tough job isn't it? Bing Bong; "Hello, can I interest you in a ... Oh you've got one already, haven't you? Well never mind ..."

- ❖ George Carlin: Ever notice that anyone going slower than you is a nincompoop, but anyone going faster is a maniac?

- Michael McIntyre: Who's phoning radio stations to warn of traffic jams? Who in their right mind gets stuck and thinks: "Get me the phone — I must warn the others. It's too late for me?"

- Phyllis Diller: I do dinner in three phases: serve the food, clear the table, bury the dead.

- Russell Brand: No wonder Bob Geldof is such an expert on famine. He's been dining off 'I Don't Like Mondays' for 30 years.

- I haven't talked to my wife in three weeks. I didn't want to interrupt her.

- People used to laugh at me when I would say "I want to be a comedian." Well, nobody's laughing now.

- My mum told me to stop impersonating a flamingo. I had to put my foot down.

- I haven't slept for three days, because that would be too long.

- The first time I got a universal remote control, I thought to myself, "This changes everything."

- My girlfriend has the heart of a lion and a lifetime ban from the local zoo.

- I refused to believe my road worker father was stealing from his job, but when I got home, all the signs were there.

- I recently decided to sell my vacuum cleaner; all it was doing was gathering dust.

- People say I'm condescending. That means I talk down to people.

- You can never lose a homing pigeon. If your homing pigeon doesn't come back, what you've lost is a pigeon.

- Whiteboards are remarkable.

- I was at an ATM and this old lady asked me to help check her balance, so I pushed her over.

- I have an inferiority complex, but it's not a very good one.

- Shout-out to all sidewalks; for keeping me off the streets.

- Love means nothing to a tennis player.

- Six out of seven dwarves are not happy.

- They took my mood ring, and I don't know how to feel about that.

- Inspecting mirrors is a job I could really see myself doing.

- I'm so hip old ladies are trying to replace me.

- I'd give my left arm to be ambidextrous.

- Words cannot express how limited my vocabulary is.

- My girlfriend likes to do this really cute thing where she doesn't exist.

- Getting paid to sleep would be a dream job.

- My fear of moving stairs is escalating.

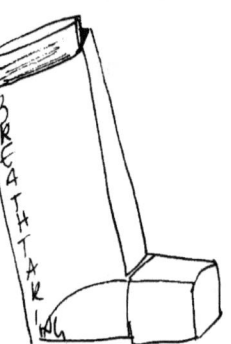

- I used to be a banker, but I lost interest.

- Asthma; it's breathtaking.

- I used to be indecisive, but now I'm not so sure.

- What do you get when you cross a rhetorical question with a joke?

"I've written a joke about a fat badger, but I couldn't fit it into my set" – Masai Graham

"Always leave them wanting more, my uncle used to say to me. Which is why he lost his job in disaster relief" – Mark Watson

"I was given some Sudoku toilet paper. It didn't work. You could only fill it in with number 1's and number 2's" – Bec Hill

"I wanted to do a show about feminism. But my husband wouldn't let me" – Ria Lina

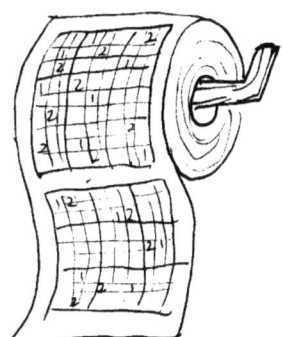

"Money can't buy you happiness? Well, check this out. I bought myself a McHappy Meal" – Paul F Taylor

"Scotland had oil, but it's running out thanks to all that deep frying" – Scott Capurro

"I've been married for ten years; I haven't made a decision for seven" – Jason Cook

"This show is about perception and perspective. But it depends how you look at it" – Felicity Ward

"I go to the kebab shop so much that when they call me boss in there, it's less a term of affection and more of an economic reality" – Ed Gamble

"Leadership looks fun, but it's stressful. Just look at someone leading a conga" – James Acaster

"I bought myself some glasses. My observational comedy improved" – Sara Pascoe

---

Two antennas met on a roof, fell in love and got married. The ceremony wasn't much, but the reception was excellent.

A jumper cable walks into a bar. The bartender says, "I'll serve you, but don't start anything."

A woman has twins and gives them up for adoption. One of them goes to a family in Egypt and is named 'Ahmal.' The other goes to a family in Spain; they name him 'Juan.' Years later, Juan sends a picture of himself to his birth mother. Upon receiving the picture, she tells her husband that she wishes she also had a picture of Ahmal. Her husband responds, "They're twins! If you've seen Juan, you've seen Ahmal."

A man walks into a bar with a slab of asphalt under his arm and says: "A beer please, and one for the road."

"Doc, I can't stop singing 'The Green, Green Grass of Home'."
"That sounds like Tom Jones Syndrome."
"Is it common?"
"Well, 'It's Not Unusual'."

An invisible man marries an invisible woman. The kids were nothing to look at either.

Deja Moo: The feeling that you've heard this bull before.
I went to buy some camouflage trousers the other day but I couldn't find any.

A man woke up in a hospital after a serious accident. He shouted, "Doctor, doctor, I can't feel my legs!" The doctor replied, "I know you can't. I've cut off your arms!"

Two fish swim into a concrete wall. One turns to the other and says, "Dam!"

Two Eskimos sitting in a kayak were chilly, so they lit a fire in the craft. Unsurprisingly, it sunk, proving once again, that you can't have your kayak and heat it too.

A group of chess enthusiasts checked into a hotel and were standing in the lobby discussing their recent tournament victories. After about an hour, the manager came out of the office and asked them to disperse. "But why," they asked, as they moved off.
"Because," he said, "I can't stand chess-nuts boasting in an open foyer."

Two peanuts walk into a bar, and one was a salted.
As you know, Mahatma Gandhi walked barefoot most of

the time, which produced an impressive set of calluses on his feet. He also ate very little, which made him rather frail and with his odd diet, he suffered from bad breath. This made him ... (Oh, man, this is so bad, it's good ...) A super calloused fragile mystic hexed by halitosis.

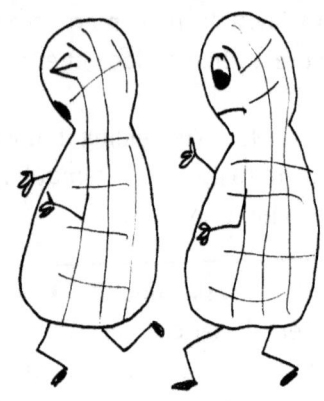

Why do cows wear bells? Because, their horns don't work.

There was the person who sent twenty different puns to his friends, with the hope that at least ten of the puns would make them laugh. No pun in ten did!

Parallel lines have so much in common. It's a shame they'll never meet.

My Grade 10 teacher accused me of being immature. I told her to get out of my fort.

Women only call me ugly until they find out how much money I make. Then they call me ugly and poor.

How many Germans does it take to screw in a light bulb? One, they're efficient and not very funny.

What do you call a dog with no legs? It doesn't matter; it's not going to come.
Someone stole my Microsoft Office and they're going to pay. You have my Word.

What's green, fuzzy, and if it fell out of a tree, it would kill you? A pool table.

Apparently, someone in London gets stabbed every 52 seconds. Poor fellow.

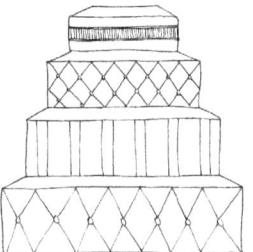

I went to a really emotional wedding the other day. Even the cake was in tiers.

We have a genetic predisposition for diarrhoea. Runs in our jeans.

Want to hear a word I just made up? Plagiarism.

What did the pirate say when he turned 80? Aye, Matey.

I took the shell off my racing snail, thinking it would make him run faster. If anything, it made him more sluggish.

I tried to catch fog yesterday. Mist.

The first rule of the Alzheimer's club is, don't talk about the Chess club.

Why does a chicken coop have two doors? If it had four doors, it would be a chicken sedan.

I told my wife she was drawing her eyebrows too high. She looked surprised.

---

1. Tell me what you need, and I'll tell you how to get along without it.

2. Accept that some days you are the pigeon and some days the statue.

3. Needing someone is like needing a parachute. If he isn't there the first time, chances are you won't need him again.

4. I don't have an attitude problem; you have a perception problem.

5. Last night, I lay in bed looking up at the stars in the sky and I thought to myself, where the heck is the ceiling?

6. My reality check bounced.

7. On the keyboard of life, always keep one finger on the escape key.

8. I don't suffer from stress. I am a carrier.

9. You are slower than a herd of turtles stampeding through peanut butter.

10. Do not meddle in the affairs of dragons, because you are crunchy and taste good with ketchup.

11. Everybody is somebody else's weirdo.

12. A pat on the back is only a few centimetres from a kick in the butt.

13. Don't be irreplaceable. If you can't be replaced, you can't be promoted.

14. After any salary raise, you will have less money at the end of the month than you did before.

15. You can go anywhere you want if you look serious and carry a clipboard.

16. Eat one live toad the first thing in the morning and nothing worse will happen to you the rest of the day.

17. If it wasn't for the last minute, nothing would get done.

18. When you don't know what to do, walk fast and look worried.

19. Following the rules will not get the job done.

20. When confronted by a difficult problem, you can solve it more easily by reducing it to the question, "How would the Lone Ranger handle this?"

21. Everyone has a photographic memory. Some just don't have film.

❖ If you ever see me getting beaten by the police, put down the video camera and come help me. – Bobcat Goldthwaite

❖ I'm a psychic amnesiac. I know in advance what I'll forget. – Michael McShane

❖ My mum said she learned how to swim. Someone took her out in the lake and threw her off the boat ... that's how she learned how to swim. I said, 'Mum, they weren't trying to teach you how to swim.' – Paula Poundstone

❖ In elementary school, in case of fire you have to line up quietly in a single file line from smallest to tallest. What is the logic? Do tall people burn slower? – Warren Hutcherson

❖ Relationships are hard. It's like a full-time job, and we should treat it like one. If your boyfriend or girlfriend wants to leave you, they should give you two weeks' notice.

There should be severance pay, and before they leave you, they should have to find you a temp. – Bob Ettinger

❖ A study in the *Washington Post* says that women have better verbal skills than men. I just want to say to the authors of that study – 'Duh!' – Conan O'Brien

❖ I had a linguistics professor who said that it's man's ability to use language that makes him the dominant species on the planet. That may be. But I think there's one other thing that separates us from animals. We aren't afraid of vacuum cleaners. – Jeff Stimson

❖ Did you ever walk in a room and forget why you walked in? I think that's how dogs spend their lives. – Sue Murphy

❖ The statistics on sanity are that one out of every four Americans is suffering from some form of mental illness. Think of your three best friends. If they are okay, then it's you. – Rita Mae Brown

❖ My grandfather's a little forgetful, but he likes to give me advice. One day, he took me aside and left me there. – Ron Richards

❖ Some women hold up dresses that are so ugly and they always say the same thing: "This looks much better on." On what? On fire? – Rita Rudner

❖ The ad in the paper said 'Big Sale. Last Week.' Why advertise? I already missed it. They're just rubbing it in. – Yakov Smirnoff

❖ *USA Today* has come out with a new survey: Apparently three out of four people make up 75 per cent of the population. – David Letterman

❖ You know how to tell if the teacher has had a long night? Movie Day. – Jay Mohr

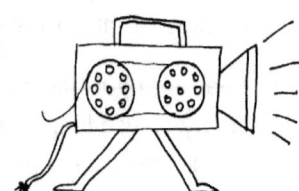

❖ I was in a supermarket and I saw Paul Newman's face on salad dressing and spaghetti sauce. I thought he was missing. – Bob Saget

❖ I just broke up with someone and the last thing she said to me was, "You'll never find anyone like me again!" I'm thinking, "I should hope not! If I don't want you, why would I want someone like you?" – Larry Miller

❖ If your parents never had children, chances are you won't either. – Dick Cavett

❖ I was a vegetarian until I started leaning towards sunlight. – Rita Rudner

❖ I always wanted to be somebody, but I should have been more specific. – Lily Tomlin

❖ The Swiss have an interesting army. Five hundred years without a war. Pretty impressive. Also, pretty

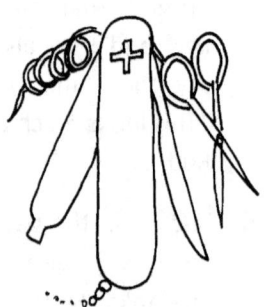

lucky for them. Ever see that little Swiss Army knife they have to fight with? Not much of a weapon there: corkscrews, bottle openers. "Come on, buddy, let's go. You get past me, the guy in back of me, he's got a spoon. Back off. I've got the toe clippers right here". – Jerry Seinfeld

❖ Why does Sea World have a seafood restaurant? I'm halfway through my fish burger and I realise, Oh no! I could be eating a slow learner. – Lynda Montgomery

❖ Sometimes I think war is just a way for world leaders to learn geography. – Paul Rodriguez

❖ Where lipstick is concerned, the important thing is not colour, but to accept where your lips end. – Jerry Seinfeld

❖ I think that's how Chicago got started. A bunch of people in New York said, "Gee, I'm enjoying the crime and the poverty, but it just isn't cold enough. Let's go west!" – Richard Jeni

---

1. Well, this day was a total waste of makeup.

2. Do I look like a people person?

3. You! Off my planet!

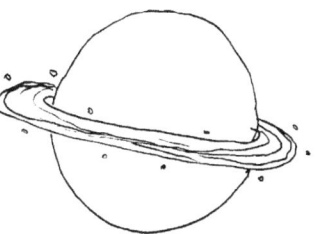

4. Therapy is expensive, popping bubble wrap is cheap. You choose.

5. Does your train of thought have a caboose?

6. See no evil, hear no evil, date no evil.

7. Sarcasm is just one more service we offer.

8. Whatever kind of look you were going for, you missed.

9. Sure it's user-friendly … if you know what you're doing.

10. I majored in liberal arts. Will that be to eat here or take away?

11. Living proof that nature does not abhor a vacuum.

12. I can't remember if I'm the good twin or the evil one.

13. I just want revenge. Is that so wrong?

14. Can I trade this job for what's behind the door?

15. I like cats, too. Let's exchange recipes.

16. Macho Law prohibits me from admitting I'm wrong.

17. Not all men are annoying. Some are dead.

18. Too many freaks, not enough circuses.

19. Chaos, panic and disorder; my work here is done.

20. Ambivalent? Well, yes and no.

21. Is it time for your medication or mine?

22. My neighbour knocked at my door at 3.00am this morning! Can you believe it? 3.00am! Luckily, I was still up playing my drums.

23. I thought I wanted a career; turns out I just wanted pay cheques.

24. I'm not tense; just terribly, terribly alert.

❖ I've just been on an once-in-a-lifetime holiday. I'll tell you what, never again – Tim Vine

❖ I used to think an ocean of soda existed, but it was just a Fanta sea – Bec Hill

❖ My wife told me: "I love you so much more on holiday." That wasn't a very nice postcard to receive – Joe Bor

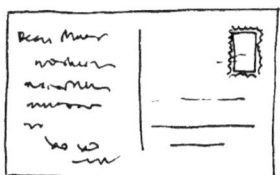

- I wonder how long it will be until airlines aren't only charging for physical baggage, but for emotional baggage too. Not that it'd bother me. I'm fine. Really! Just ask my dad. Who's never there! – Tegan Higginbotham

- Have you heard about the evil group of men who control all of the world's cheese? The hallouminati. – Nick Helm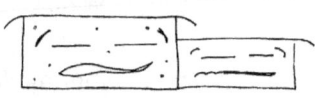

- When my wife and I argue, we're like a band in concert: we start with some new stuff, and then we roll out our greatest hits – Frank Skinner

---

A woman was reporting her car as stolen and mentioned that there was a car phone in it. The policeman taking the report called the phone and told the guy that answered that he had read the ad in the newspaper and wanted to buy the car. They arranged to meet, and the thief was arrested.

5
Q&A

Q: How many lawyers does it take to change a light bulb?

A: Whereas the party of the first part, also known as 'Lawyer', and the party of the second part, also known as 'Light Bulb', do hereby and forthwith agree to a transaction wherein the party of the second part (Light Bulb) shall be removed from the current position as a result of failure to perform previously agreed upon duties, i.e. the lighting, elucidation, and otherwise illumination of the area ranging from the front (north) door, through the entryway, terminating at an area just inside the primary living area, demarcated by the beginning of the carpet, any spill over illumination being at the option of the party of the second part (Light Bulb), and not required by the aforementioned agreement between the parties. The aforementioned

removal transaction shall include, but not be limited to, the following steps:

1. The party of the first part (Lawyer) shall, with or without elevation at his option, by means of a chair, step stool, ladder or any other means of elevation, grasp the party of the second part (Light Bulb) and rotate the party of the second part (Light Bulb) in a counter-clockwise direction, this point being non-negotiable.

2. Upon reaching a point where the party of the second part (Light Bulb) becomes separated from the party of the third part ('Receptacle'), the party of the first part (Lawyer), shall have the option of disposing of the party of the second part (Light Bulb) in a manner consistent with all applicable state, local, and federal statutes.

3. Once separation and disposal have been achieved, the party of the first part (Lawyer) shall have the option of commencing installation of the party of the fourth part ('New Light Bulb'). This installation shall occur in a manner consistent with the reverse of the procedures described in step one of this self-same document, being careful to note that the rotation should occur in a clockwise direction, this point also being non-negotiable.

Note: The above described steps may be performed, at the option of the party of the first part (Lawyer), by any or all persons authorised by him, the objective being to produce the most possible revenue for the party of the fifth part, also known as 'Partnership'.

Why Did the Chicken Cross the Road?

- ❖ Pat Buchanan: To steal a job from a decent, hardworking American.

- ❖ Colonel Sanders: I missed one?

- ❖ LA Police Department: Give us five minutes with the chicken and we'll find out.

- ❖ Dr Seuss: Did the chicken cross the road? Did he cross it with a toad? Yes, the chicken crossed the road. But why it crossed, I've not been told!

- ❖ Ernest Hemingway: To die. In the rain.

- ❖ Martin Luther King Jr.: I envision a world where all chickens will be free to cross roads without having their motives called into question.

- ❖ Grandpa: In my day, we didn't ask why the chicken crossed the road. Someone told us that the chicken crossed the road, and that was good enough for us.

- ❖ Aristotle: It is the nature of chickens to cross the road.

- ❖ Karl Marx: It was an historical inevitability.

- Ronald Reagan: What chicken?

- Captain James T. Kirk: To boldly go where no chicken has gone before.

- Fox Mulder: You saw it cross with your own eyes. How many more chickens have to cross before you believe it?

- Machiavelli: The point is that the chicken crossed the road. Who cares why? The end of crossing the road justifies whatever motive there was.

- Bill Gates: I have just released 'Chicken Coop 98', which will not only cross roads, but will lay eggs, file your important documents, and balance your chequebook, and Explorer is an inextricable part of the operating system.

- Einstein: Did the chicken really cross the road or did the road move beneath the chicken?

- Kindergarten teacher: To get to the other side.

- Plato: For the greater good.

- Timothy Leary: Because that is the only trip the establishment would let it take.

- Ronald Reagan: I forget.

- Hippocrates: Because of an excess of phlegm in its pancreas.

❖ PriceWaterhouseCoopers: Deregulation of the chicken's side of the road was threatening its dominant market position. The chicken was faced with significant challenges to create and develop the competencies required for the newly competitive market. PriceWaterhouseCoopers, in a partnering relationship with the client, helped the chicken by rethinking its physical distribution strategy and implantation processes. Using the Poultry Integration Model (PIM), PriceWaterhouseCoopers helped the chicken use its skills, methodologies, knowledge, capital and experiences to align the chicken's people processes and technology in support of its overall strategy within the Program Management framework.

o PriceWaterhouseCoopers convened a diverse cross-spectrum of road analysts and best chickens, along with PriceWaterhouseCoopers consultants with deep skills in the transportation industry, to engage in a two-hour itinerary of meetings in order to leverage their person knowledge capital (both tacit and explicit) and to enable them to synergise with each other in order to achieve the implicit goals of delivering and successfully architecting and implementing an enterprises-wide value framework across the continuum of poultry cross-median processes.

o The meeting was held in a park-like setting, enabling and creating an impactful environment which was strategically based, industry-focused and built upon a consistent, clear and unified market message and aligned with the chicken's mission, vision and core values. This was conducive towards the creation of a total business integration solution.

- o PricewaterhouseCoopers helped the chicken's change to become more successful...

❖ Richard M Nixon: The chicken did not cross the road. I repeat, the chicken did NOT cross the road.

❖ Jerry Seinfeld: Why does anyone cross the road? I mean, why doesn't anyone ever think to ask, "What the heck was this chicken doing walking around all over the place anyway?"

❖ Oliver Stone: The question is not, "Why did the chicken cross the road?" Rather, it is, "Who was crossing the road at the same time, who did we overlook in our haste to observe the chicken crossing?"

❖ Darwin: Chickens, over great periods of time, have been naturally selected in such a way that they are now genetically disposed to cross roads.

❖ Buddha: Asking this question denies your own chicken nature.

❖ Ralph Waldo Emerson: The chicken did not cross the road. It transcended it.

- Why does the sun lighten our hair, but darken our skin?

- Why can't women put on mascara with their mouth closed?

- Why doesn't glue stick to the inside of the bottle?

- Why don't you ever see the headline: 'Psychic Wins Lottery'?

- Why is 'abbreviated' such a long word?

- Why is a boxing ring square?

- Why is it called lipstick if you can still move your lips?

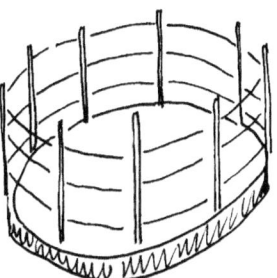

- Why is it considered necessary to nail down the lid of a coffin?

- Why is it that doctors and lawyers call what they do 'practice'?

- Why is it that rain drops but snow falls?

- Why is it that to stop Windows, you have to click on 'Start'?

- Why is it that when you're driving and looking for an address, you turn down the volume on the radio?

- Why is lemon juice made with artificial flavour and dishwashing liquid made with real lemons?

- Why is the person who invests your money, called a broker?

- Why is the third hand on a watch, called a 'second hand'?

- Why is the time of day with the slowest traffic, called 'rush hour'?

- Why is the word 'dictionary' in the dictionary?

- Why isn't there a special name for the tops of your feet?

- You know that little indestructible black box that is used on planes. Why can't they make the whole plane out of the same substance?

The defence attorney was cross-examining a police officer during a felony trial. It went like this:

Q.: Officer, did you see my client fleeing the scene?

A.: No sir, but I subsequently observed a person matching the description of the offender running several blocks away.

Q.: Officer, who provided this description?

A.: The officer who responded to the scene.

Q.: A fellow officer provided the description of this so-called offender. Do you trust your fellow officers?

A.: Yes sir, with my life.

Q.: With your life? Let me ask you this question then officer. Do you have a locker room in the police station – a room where you change your clothes in preparation for your daily duties?

A.: Yes sir, we do.

Q.: And do you have a locker in that room?

A.: Yes sir, I do.

Q.: And do you have a lock on your locker?

A.: Yes sir.

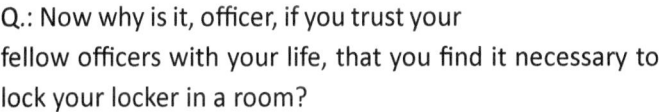

Q.: Now why is it, officer, if you trust your fellow officers with your life, that you find it necessary to lock your locker in a room?

A.: Sometimes lawyers have been known to walk through that room.

With that, the courtroom erupted in laughter, and a prompt recess was called. The officer on the stand has been nominated for this year's best comeback line.

This is an actual job application a 17-year-old boy submitted at a fast-food establishment, and they hired him because he was so honest and funny!

NAME: Greg Bulmash.

DESIRED POSITION: Company's President or Vice President. But seriously, whatever's available. If I was in a position to be picky, I wouldn't be applying here in the first place.

DESIRED SALARY: $185,000 a year plus stock options and a huge CEO style-severance package. If that's not possible, make an offer and we can haggle.

EDUCATION: Yes.

LAST POSITION HELD: Target for middle-management hostility.

SALARY: Less than I'm worth.

MOST NOTABLE ACHIEVEMENT: My incredible collection of stolen pens and Post-It notes.

REASON FOR LEAVING: It sucked.

HOURS AVAILABLE TO WORK: Any.

PREFERRED HOURS: 1.30–3.30 pm, Monday, Tuesday and Thursday.

DO YOU HAVE ANY SPECIAL SKILLS?: Yes, but they're better suited to the sporting field.

MAY WE CONTACT YOUR CURRENT EMPLOYER?: If I had one, would I be here?

DO YOU HAVE ANY PHYSICAL CONDITIONS THAT WOULD PROHIBIT YOU FROM LIFTING UP TO 50 LBS?: Of what?

DO YOU HAVE A CAR?: I think the more appropriate question here would be, 'Do you have a car that runs?'

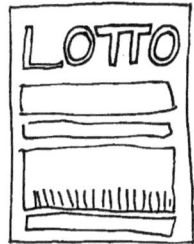

HAVE YOU RECEIVED ANY SPECIAL AWARDS OR RECOGNITION?: I may already be a winner of the Publishers Clearing House Sweepstakes.

WHAT WOULD YOU LIKE TO BE DOING IN FIVE YEARS?: Living in the Bahamas, retired, without a care in the world. Actually, I'd like to be doing that now.

DO YOU CERTIFY THAT THE ABOVE IS TRUE AND COMPLETE TO THE BEST OF YOUR KNOWLEDGE?: Yes. Absolutely.

SIGN HERE: Aries.

Other books from the Words from Daddy's Mouth Studio

Early Childhood Readers (ages 4 – 6)

Broken Bones
When my dad was little, he had an old yellow bike.
But his friend's bike, which was new, was a red racer.

Find out what happens when dad swaps his bike with his friend in *Broken Bones*.

Radio Competitions
When my dad was little, he liked to listen to the radio.
Sometimes the radio station had competitions.

Find out what happens when dad tries to win a prize in *Radio Competitions*.

The Sports Room
When my dad was little, he used to help look after the school sports room.
Some of his friends helped too.
Find out what happens when dad puts away the sports equipment in *The Sports Room*.

The Ball Game

When my dad was little, he liked to play ball games.

One game, called 'Brandings', was like hide-and-seek.

Find out what happens when dad plays 'Brandings' in *The Ball Game*.

Younger Readers (ages 7 – 10)

Book One
The Big Rusty Nail

The Big Rusty Nail is an entertaining journey of a day in the life of a primary school sports room monitor, shared between a dad and his young children.

The story also provides a modern take on the proverb 'A Stitch in Time Saves Nine.' That is, stopping something before it happens is often better than having to fix things up after the event.

Book Two
The Terrible Red Racer
What happens when Dad swaps his yellow BMX bike for his friend's red racer? Find out in the latest 'Words from Daddy's Mouth'— The Terrible Red Racer. The story also provides a modern take on 'Murphy's Law.' That is, what can go wrong, will go wrong.

Book Three
The Weekend Cash Call
Find out about some of the things that dad has won from radio competitions in the latest book from the 'Words from Daddy's mouth' series - 'The Weekend Cash Call.' The story provides a modern take on the proverb that 'Fortune favours the brave.'

Book Four
The Brandings Game
For Dad, there was something even worse than the Terrible Red Racer and this was 'The Brandings Game' - the latest book in the Words from Daddy's Mouth series.

The story provides a modern take on the proverb 'Look before you leap.'

Chapter Books (ages 7 – 10)

Book Five
The Most Amazing Golf Shot Ever

Golf was another sport that Dad was really good at; or was he? Find out in the latest 'Words from Daddy's Mouth' release - 'The Most Amazing Golf Shot Ever.'

The story provides a modern take on 'Practice makes perfect.'

Book Six
Undercover Cop

Find out how Dad became the centre of a criminal investigation, while working in a city shop in the latest book from the 'Words from Daddy's Mouth' series – 'Undercover Cop.'

The story also provides a modern take on 'Don't judge a book by its cover.'

Book Seven
The Dead Lawn Incident

Before Dad could become a lawnmower man, he had to get the lawn to survive – find out if he could in the latest instalment of the 'Words from Daddy's Mouth' series 'The Dead Lawn Incident.'

The story provides a modern take on the proverb 'You reap what you sow.'

Coming Soon   **Book Eight**
Crashing into a Police Car
Dad has ever only owned one car in his whole life, and it was never the same after 'Crashing into a Police Car' – the latest instalment from the 'Words from Daddy's Mouth' series.

The story provides a modern take on 'More haste, less speed.'

For Parents and Teachers

The Complete Guide to books 1 to 4 from the 'Words from Daddy's Mouth' Series
The team at Words from Daddy's Mouth have developed a notes and worksheets book that serves as a complementary kit for teachers, parents and tutors to assist with giving young readers a head start.

The book contains numerous practical tips, games and insights to learning techniques.

Enjoy easy access to the comprehensive and tailored reading collateral, with material for all of the first four books in the series conveniently consolidated in one place in this book titled - 'The Complete Guide to books 1 to 4 from the Words from Daddy's Mouth series.'

About how this all began (and why Lily Burgess is the author on the cover of the books)

By Matthew Burgess

Being a full time lawyer I needed a creative outlet, and in 2010, began writing business books for other professional service providers.

However there was still something missing. My wife said she married me because I made her laugh with the crazy stories I told her when we first met and that I should write a book.

Many years later we began to raise one, then two, then three and finally four precious girls and I started to share stories of my childhood with them.

It soon became one of our family's favourite pastimes listening to these stories about my childhood. Often embellished and seldom kept on track, the girls would be absorbed. What was fact became blurred in the magic of the stories told.

There is a strong undertone in these stories which carry various life lessons, while also ensuring a healthy dose of humour and role playing.

When my third daughter, Lily, was about four years old, she said, "Daddy, please tell me another story from your mouth."

From that day on, the stories became known as "Words from Daddy's mouth." It was therefore a natural progression that Lily Burgess would become the pseudonym for the authoring of my children books to help distinguish them from my other publications.

With so many stories, we had to create a list to remember them all (at last count the list was nearing 500). So over time a game developed where the girls would choose a number from the list. Whatever story related to the number chosen would be the story that I would tell.

Stories were usually told as the last part of the wind down of an evening, sitting together in a bedroom or on a lounge chair.

I hope you enjoy sharing the stories with your children.

Matthew (and Lily) Burgess

© 2014 Bambini Talent Group

www.ingramcontent.com/pod-product-compliance
Lightning Source LLC
LaVergne TN
LVHW020934090426
835512LV00020B/3356